MORAL KNOWLEDGE

MORAL KNOWLEDGE

by

OLIVER A. JOHNSON

University of California, Riverside

MARTINUS NIJHOFF / THE HAGUE 1966

V9299
BJ1471 J6

TO MY MOTHER AND FATHER

PREFACE

As its title indicates, this book is concerned with two different fields of philosophy, ethics and epistemology. The bulk of the argument is devoted to epistemological questions, as these arise within the context of morality. Hence, the conclusions I reach could probably best be described as prolegomena to the elaboration of a theory of ethics. I have plans, which I hope will be realized in the next few years, of elaborating such a theory.

I started work on *Moral Knowledge* in the summer of 1958 with the help of a University Faculty Fellowship, for which I am most grateful. Much of the research for the book, as well as a good bit of its writing, was done in two libraries, The University Library, Berkeley, and the Bodleian Library, Oxford. Members of the staffs of both libraries, by their courtesy and helpfulness, lightened immeasurably the task of my research. I owe a special debt of gratitude to four people—to Mr. George Caukwell, Fellow of University College, and Mr. W. H. Walsh, Fellow of Merton College (now Professor in the University of Edinburgh), whose hospitality and generosity brought welcome warmth to our winter in Oxford, and to my colleagues in philosophy at UCR, Professors Philip Wheelwright and Peter Fuss, both of whom read the manuscript with sympathetic but critically scrutinizing eyes. Their perceptive comments helped rescue the book from some of the more egregious lapses of the manuscript. Finally, I should like to thank Mrs. Betty Harker and Miss Eleanore Stone for their work in typing the manuscript.

Quotations appear in the book from *Mind*, from *The Philosophical Quarterly*, from *Proceedings of the British Academy*, from *The Twentieth Century* and from various publications of Basil Blackwell, Cambridge University Press, The Clarendon Press, Macmillan and Company, Oxford University Press, Penguin Books, and the Tudor Publishing Company. Grateful acknowledgment is made for these.

Riverside   September, 1965

TABLE OF CONTENTS

CHAPTER I

THE PROBLEM OF MORAL KNOWLEDGE

Very few people are moral cynics. Although many people scoff at some, or even most of the moral customs of our society, almost everyone, no matter how depraved he may appear to be, has convictions about what he ought and ought not to do. He draws some moral line beyond which he will not go; or, if he does violate it, he condemns himself for having done wrong. According to an old saying "There is honor even among thieves." The proverb is an overstatement; nevertheless it does, I think, contain this much truth, that a totally depraved human being is rarely found.

Although moral cynics may be rare, moral skeptics abound. For many people, though they have convictions about the way in which they ought to live and act (hence are not cynics), have come to the skeptical conclusion that it is impossible to provide any rational foundation for these convictions. Such people believe that they have duties but find themselves unable to give any good reasons in support of their beliefs. So they conclude that, no matter how firmly they hold their moral beliefs to be true, they cannot know them to be so. Such skeptical doubts about the possibility of knowing whether our beliefs about what we ought to do are true pose the problem: *Can* we provide any good reasons for these moral convictions? The issue raised by this question I shall call the problem of moral knowledge. My object in this book will be to try to find a solution to it.

It should be noted that my concern in the book is a quite specific one; I am seeking reasons capable of supporting our beliefs about our duties (or about what we morally ought to do) in order to justify the conclusion that we can know that some beliefs of this kind are true. To call such a limited issue *the* problem of moral knowledge, it might be suggested, is to take a one-sided view of ethics, which leaves out of consideration the problem of knowledge of the Good, famous among moral philosophers since Plato. I shall not attempt here to defend my selection of problems but shall only say that the issue with which I shall be concerned is *a* problem of moral knowledge, and an extremely important one. I believe personally that it is the most important problem of ethical theory and hope that what I have to say in the book will bear out my belief.

1. CONTEMPORARY SOURCES OF MORAL SKEPTICISM

The problem of moral knowledge is not new. Since Socrates tried to rehabilitate moral philosophy following the skeptical attacks of the Sophists, the issue has risen over and over again in the history of Western thought. Although later moral skeptics have posed serious objections to the possibility of moral knowledge, probably none has succeeded in gaining for his skeptical views the kind of ascendency achieved by the Sophists in fifth-century Greece. Not, that is, until the twentieth century. Today, however, we find the skeptical position accepted by many highly respected moral theorists. The current prominence of moral skepticism rests on several grounds; to a considerable extent it stems from a number of powerful attacks that have been mounted against traditional moral thought from outside of philosophy itself. The first of these is cultural relativism, which, though as old as the Sophists, has received new vigor and persuasiveness from the detailed researches of modern anthropologists. The second kind of contemporary moral skepticism is new, arising out of the work in depth psychology of Freud and his successors. A third (and in certain respects ambivalent) source of skepticism, the dialectical materialism of the Marxists, has a quasi-philosophical origin. Finally, from within philosophy itself, has come a vigorous attack on the possibility of moral knowledge. The logical positivists, through the use of the verification principle, have succeeded, at least to their own satisfaction, in excluding assertions about what we ought to do from the realm of cognitive meaningfulness.

Since my purpose in this book will be to provide a justification for moral knowledge, I shall oppose the conclusions of the moral skeptics, whatever the source of their skepticism may be. However, I do not intend to discuss or to examine the arguments advanced by the contemporary skeptics whom I have just mentioned. My reasons for not doing so are two: First, the theories I have referred to have been canvassed, both pro and con, so thoroughly in the last several years by moral philosophers that I doubt that I could at this late date add anything of consequence to the discussion. Secondly, and more important, there exists a quite different critique of the possibility of moral knowledge, which I have not yet mentioned, but which, unless it can be met, succeeds in a simple yet devastating way in eliminating any possibility of my giving an affirmative answer to the question that I have posed for myself in this book. Unless the argument I shall now turn to can be answered, the possibility of moral knowledge cannot, I believe, be shown. On the other hand, if this argument can be answered, it is possible that moral knowledge can be vindicated in such a measure that the objections raised by all the other skeptics can be dismissed without further consideration. The argument I am referring to, characteristically enough, comes from Hume.

2. HUME AND THE DEDUCTIVE FALLACY

In Book III of his *Treatise of Human Nature* Hume writes as follows: "In every system of morality, which I have hitherto met with, I have always remark'd, that the author proceeds for some time in the ordinary way of reasoning, and establishes the being of a God, or makes observations concerning human affairs; when of a sudden I am surpriz'd to find, that instead of the usual copulations of propositions, *is*, and *is not*, I meet with no proposition that is not connected with an *ought*, or an *ought not*. This change is imperceptible; but is, however, of the last consequence. For as this *ought*, or *ought not* expresses some new relation or affirmation, 'tis necessary that it shou'd be observ'd and explain'd; and at the same time that a reason should be given, for what seems altogether inconceivable, how this new relation can be a deduction from others, which are entirely different from it. But as authors do not commonly use this precaution, I shall presume to recommend it to the readers; and am persuaded, that this small attention wou'd subvert all the vulgar systems of morality..."[1]

At first glance Hume's criticism of the arguments of the moral philosophers may appear innocuous and one is somewhat taken aback by the sweeping statement with which he ends it. Actually his conclusion is a model of understatement; for he has, with typical Humean precision, put his finger on the one weak spot capable of subverting not just the "vulgar" systems of morality but even some of the most

---

[1] David Hume, *A Treatise of Human Nature*, Book III, Part I, Sect. I. There has been considerable disagreement recently about just what Hume himself intended by this argument. Since my interest in the argument is a philosophical rather than a scholarly one, I shall not enter into the controversy.

sophisticated theories that the finest philosophical minds, both before and after his time, have been able to devise. To see why Hume's argument is so devastating, it will be necessary to develop it a step further than he has himself done. The effect of his argument is to confront moral philosophers with an apparently inescapable dilemma. The issue may be put in the following way: Moral philosophers have made it their object to formulate theories of moral obligation. They believe that there are certain kinds of acts that we ought (or ought not) to do. Their theories represent attempts to provide a rational justification for these beliefs so that we can accept them, not simply arbitrarily as a matter of faith, but as legitimate items of knowledge. In other words, these philosophers try to provide good reasons for our convictions about our duties. The reasons they give, if they are to qualify as good (or justifying) reasons, must *lead to* the conclusion we draw from them. Or, looked at from the other side, if the reasons they give in support of a conclusion are to qualify as good reasons, then the conclusion must *follow from* those reasons. What, then, is the relationship between reasons and conclusion that I have referred to by the metaphorical expressions "lead to" and "follow from"? It is logical, or deductive entailment. For a set of premises (reasons) to "lead to" a given conclusion, they must logically entail that conclusion; for a conclusion to "follow from" a set of premises (reasons), it must be logically entailed by them.

But in the kind of argument we are concerned with here the conclusion we wish to justify is an assertion of moral obligation, a statement containing a moral "ought." The reasons that we give in its support must themselves either contain or not contain a moral "ought" as well. Logically, these alternatives are exhaustive. If the reasons do not contain a moral "ought"—and this is the side of the dilemma that Hume presents—then they cannot be good reasons for the conclusion that is derived from them. For logically they do not entail that conclusion. To derive a conclusion containing an "ought" from a set of premises that do not contain an "ought" is to be guilty of a *non sequitur*. If, on the other hand, the justifying premises do contain a moral "ought," the desired conclusion can legitimately be drawn. However, we are then left with an unjustified moral "ought," the one in the premises, which must be justified before the conclusion we are attempting to establish can possibly qualify as an item of knowledge. To justify this "ought" we need a further argument, and a further, and so on. The result is that either we are forced into an infinite regress or at some point in the proceedings we commit a *non sequitur*. In neither case do we justify our conclusion. The consequence seems inescapable: On logical grounds alone it can be demonstrated that it is impossible to give any reasons capable of justifying a conclusion that asserts a moral obligation. Since no such conclusion can be rationally justified, none can qualify as an item of knowledge. Hence moral knowledge is impossible and the truth of the skeptics' position is firmly established. As Hume himself concluded "... morality is not an object of reason."[1]

The problem facing us, if we are to have any hope of avoiding skepticism, is to devise a theory of moral obligation which will provide a justification for our convictions about what we ought to do that can escape Hume's criticism, as I have just elaborated it. To introduce a term that I shall use throughout the book, our theory must not commit the "deductive fallacy," which I shall define as the fallacy involved in any deductive argument whose conclusion contains a moral "ought" but whose premises do not. In Hume's terms, any attempt to deduce an "ought" from an "is" commits the deductive fallacy.[2] The present book is by no means the first attempt to find an answer to Hume. On the contrary, many moral philosophers, particularly during the twentieth century, have tried to devise a theory that could justify our moral convictions without either committing a *non sequitur* or becoming trapped in an infinite regress. The examination of these theories, to which I shall devote the next several chapters, if it shows nothing else should demonstrate the extraordinary difficulty of the task.

Before going further, we should note one important feature of Hume's argument. His charge that all attempts to provide reasons justifying our beliefs about what we ought to do commit the deductive fallacy itself rests on an assumption, namely, that such justifying arguments must be *deductive* in nature. If this assumption is not correct, we may be able to elude him by employing another kind of justifying argument. But what kind would it be? The obvious alternative is an inductive type of argument. Let us see what can be done

---

[1] *Ibid.*

[2] I realize that the term "... fallacy" is out of favor today, for the good reason that philosophers have sometimes used it in referring to arguments with which they disagreed, thus relieving themselves of the necessity of having to refute those arguments. I do not intend to use it in that way. If a philosopher can show (as at least one we shall examine attempts to do) that an argument can commit the "deductive fallacy" and yet not be fallacious, I shall drop the term. In other words, one of our tasks in the book will be to decide whether the "deductive fallacy," which certainly looks like a fallacy, really is one.

with it. Inductive arguments are used to derive general conclusions from a limited set of data. We observe, perhaps, that all swans we have encountered or have read about or heard described are white, so we generalize to reach the inductive conclusion that all swans are white. Although the evidence we have to support our conclusion does not establish its truth, yet it can be argued that it gives us some (and in certain cases very good) reason for believing the conclusion to be true. Now if we could use an inductive argument in the case we are concerned with we might be able to provide reasons which, though not conclusive, might nonetheless give strong support for our conclusions about what we ought to do. But will an inductive argument work here? To argue inductively it is necessary to have, as a starting point, at least some evidence for the existence of whatever we are going to assert in our conclusion. In the illustration cited, to reach the conclusion that all swans are white—or even, with the aid of an added deductive argument, that a swan, not yet encountered, will turn out to be white—we must have some prior experience of white swans. But that is just what we do not have in the case of moral obligation. We have experience only of people (including ourselves) believing that there are moral obligations. What we are trying to establish is that these beliefs can be true. And we have no evidence whatever on which we can base any conclusion that our beliefs in the existence of moral obligations are true. For these beliefs in moral obligation, which do form a part of our experience, cannot, of themselves, establish the existence of that which they believe to exist. So we have no basis on which to make inductive generalizations. Furthermore, an inductive argument is capable of establishing only an empirical conclusion. But the case that we must make here, namely, that people really do have duties, is not an empirical one at all.

I think we must admit that the problem we are facing is one that no inductive type of argument can solve. However, we still might hope to avoid Hume's attack by devising some other kind of argument, neither inductive nor deductive, to solve the problem. Certainly this is a possibility and one that we shall have to pursue further in the course of the book. At this stage of the proceedings, however, a realization that our problem cannot be dealt with by inductive methods should serve as a warning of the extreme difficulties ahead and should make us even more aware of the devastating force of Hume's deceptively simple-sounding observations about the moral reasoning of the "vulgar."

3. THE MEANING OF MORAL OBLIGATION

I have set out the objective of this book in very general terms—to develop a theory of moral knowledge that will provide an alternative to skepticism by giving a rational justification of moral obligation capable of withstanding the logical objections of Hume. Before beginning, however, I should specify more fully and precisely just what the issue to be resolved is. We are concerned, I have said, with the problem of *moral knowledge*. Both of the terms I have italicized need considerable elucidation. I shall take them in turn.

Already in this chapter I have used the terms "obligation," "duty," and "ought." These are words with which we are all very familiar. In our ordinary discourse we use them interchangeably. We might express the same thought by saying either "I have an *obligation* to do act X," "It is my *duty* to do act X," or "I *ought* to do act X." Although certain distinctions can be drawn between the meanings of the three terms, these distinctions are quite minor. Since they would have no effect on the argument of this book I shall disregard them and shall assume the equivalence of all three terms. What, then, do the words mean? We might begin with the generalization that they are moral words and that the three equivalent statements in which I have just used them are moral assertions. However, this generalization must be qualified, for the mere presence of one of these terms in an assertion does not guarantee that the assertion is a moral one. This fact can easily be illustrated by the word "ought." Although "ought" is sometimes used as a moral expression, it is not always so used. We must make a distinction, which is a commonplace among moral philosophers, between the moral and the non-moral uses of "ought." Philosophers generally distinguish two non-moral uses of "ought," speaking of the *logical* and the *prudential* "ought" or—in Kantian terms—of "rules of skill" and "counsels of prudence." When I say "I ought to do act X" I may have nothing peculiarly moral in mind at all. For I may mean that my performance of act X is a necessary condition for the achievement of some further non-moral or even immoral end. To borrow an illustration of Kant's, if I want to poison someone, I *ought* to use a sufficient amount of an effective poison. Here the "ought" is the logical "ought." Or I may mean that by performing act X I shall satisfy some personal interest. Here the "ought" is the prudential "ought."

But there is another, moral use of "ought," which differs from both of these. When I say "I *ought* to do act X," meaning that I recognize that I have a duty or moral obligation to perform the act, I imply both that the act is itself a moral act (thus distinguishing the moral "ought" from the logical "ought") and that my obligation to perform it is independent of whether my doing so will satisfy my own interests (thus distinguishing the moral "ought" from the prudential "ought").

It is with the moral "ought," the "ought" of moral obligation, that we shall be concerned. But just what is the moral "ought"? What does it mean to say that a person has a moral obligation to do a certain act or that that act is his duty? We all use these expressions constantly but just what do we mean by them? Most moral philosophers have failed to answer these questions, seeming to prefer to operate on the assumption that it is not necessary for them to analyze the basic concepts with which they are concerned. The most notable exception is Kant; but his definition of duty, besides being extraordinarily abstract, seems hardly to be a disinterested description of the meaning that most of us would attach to the term but rather a stipulation of the meaning that he believes it must have if duty is to be a reality at all. Perhaps the difficulty that one encounters in trying to define these concepts is, as some philosophers would insist, that they are indefinable. Like such concepts as "good," or "yellow," or "one" they are simple, ultimate notions that cannot be analyzed in terms of anything else but whose meaning all of us can grasp by a direct act of intuition.

Support seems to be lent to the indefinability thesis by the problems that arise in any attempt to explicate these terms as we use them in our ordinary discourse. When talking moral language, we commonly say "I *have* a duty (or moral obligation) to do that act." Our language here is metaphorical; a duty is something that we "have" or "possess." But in what sense, if any, can we *have* a duty? Certainly we do not have it in the way that we have an apple, or even a headache. I think our ordinary usage here is misleading because the metaphor it employs makes a "thing" out of duty (like an apple), but duty is not really a thing at all, hence we cannot "have" it in the same sense that we have things. Other ordinary locutions seem only to compound the confusion. We often say "I am *under* an obligation to do that act." Here we seem to adopt a spatial metaphor; what we can be *under* must be capable of occupying space above our heads. Yet no one would seriously maintain that our duties take up space. Or, again, we sometimes say "I am morally *bound* to do that act." But once more the metaphor is inappropriate for an essential feature of bondage is missing from the situation. A person who says he is morally *bound* to do an act considers himself to be in some significant sense free. For he believes that he does not have to do the act that he says he is bound to do.[1]

Rather than trying to explicate the meaning of duty by an examination of the way in which the term is actually used in ordinary discourse, I suggest that we can get much better results if we shift our perspective somewhat. Instead of asking, "How do people ordinarily use the word 'duty'?" let us ask, "In what situations or contexts do they use this kind of language, and why?" What is there about human life and social relationships that gives rise to such linguistic forms as "ought," "duty," and "obligation"? Briefly, I think, the answer is this: Human beings, like the other animals, have various needs, desires, and inclinations. When they want something ordinarily they take it. But often two people want the same thing—or their desires clash in some other way. The result is conflict, which on the animal level is resolved by strength or cunning. Humans, however, are creatures of reason as well as desire. They have the ability to adjudicate disputes rationally. Thus, when someone takes something that I want or does some act that thwarts my desires, I demand that he give reasons for what he has done. If I am satisfied that the reasons he gives are good reasons (and if I respond rationally rather than emotionally), I concede the disputed object to him. And he does the same with me.

I suggest that the notion of moral obligation can best be understood if we approach it from the context of the reasons that people give to justify against the claims of others the acts that they do. Thus, when we say that a person has a duty to do a certain act we do not mean that he possesses some strange entity called a "duty" but rather that, in the situation in question, he can give no good reasons for not doing the act. Or when we say, to use a variant expression, that he ought, or ought not to do the act, we mean that he can give no good reasons, in the first instance, for not doing it, and, in the second, for doing it. (I am giving here only a very brief—and incomplete—preliminary analysis; I shall develop these suggestions more fully later in the book.)

I think that the approach I am suggesting succeeds in eliminating a great deal of confusion, as well as mystery, from these basic moral concepts. In addition, it has the merit of finding their meaning through an appeal to the concrete situations in life that give rise to their use

---

[1] This subject could be pursued much further, being quite interesting in itself. However, I do not think that doing so would help us much with our problem of understanding what we mean by these moral concepts. I should add that although ordinary usage, if examined carefully, proves misleading, I shall continue to use it in this book. I think that I would only increase communication difficulties if I were to abandon it.

and, I would add also, give them their significance. Finally, this method of analysis has a consequence that seems particularly consonant with our non-philosophical moral thinking. This lies in the distinction that it draws between duty, on the one hand, and desire and inclination, on the other. However little more they might be able to say about the matter, everyone would, I think, insist on distinguishing between what we want to do and what we ought to do. Our duty, they would say, is independent of our desires and any theory that attempts to reduce duty to desire explains morality finally by explaining it away. The importance people attach to this distinction becomes understandable when we focus our attention on the origin of our moral concepts. These are formulated and morality developed because men, having reason, are able by its use to recognize and in part to adopt principles of action that not only oppose but also sit in judgment on their animal impulses. To make our recognition of duty some form of desire, thus, is to obliterate the vital difference distinguishing man from the animals and making him the morally conscious being that he is and they can never be.

The analysis of duty in terms of the justification of our acts that I have just given raises several questions. One, in particular, seems immediately apparent. If we are to comprehend the idea of duty in terms of the justifications we give for what we do, how do we know that a reason we give for an act is a *good* reason? Just what is a good reason and what makes it good? These questions are crucial but they cannot be answered here because the problems they raise are essential parts of the general problem of moral knowledge. Most of the rest of the book will be devoted to an attempt to find answers to them. Before we can go on to the argument, however, we must clarify our second main concept. If we are to solve the problem of moral knowledge, we must be clear what we mean by *knowledge*.

4. THE CRITERIA OF KNOWLEDGE

I do not intend to discuss the meaning of knowledge at any length here. That would be impossible. What I shall do is to set forth, provisionally, certain criteria that a belief (or assertion or proposition) must satisfy if it is to qualify as an item of knowledge. I shall use these criteria as a general guide for the argument that follows but, as that argument develops in the course of the book, we may find it desirable to alter the criteria or, at least, to state them more fully and precisely.

The criteria that I shall use may be put in the form of *necessary* and *sufficient* conditions for knowledge.

(1) *Necessary condition.* For a belief to be an item of knowledge it is necessary that that belief be true. My conviction that it is my duty to do a certain act can qualify as an item of knowledge *only* if it is my duty to do that act. This condition for knowledge may seem too obvious to need mention; I include it because there are some contemporary philosophers who would not, I think, accept it as a necessary condition for knowledge, holding instead that one can legitimately assert that he knows something even though what he believes is in fact false. It would be beside the point here to discuss this conception of knowledge for, whatever its merits may be, I could not adopt it to fulfil the objective I have set for myself in this book, namely, to provide an alternative to moral skepticism. For, although it might be possible to find a skeptic who would be willing to grant that a moral belief could constitute an item of knowledge even though it were false, most skeptics—including both Hume and the principal philosophical exponents of moral skepticism today—would not. Since it is skeptics like these that my arguments must be designed to convince, I have to employ knowledge criteria that they will find acceptable.

(2) *Sufficient condition.* For a belief to be an item of knowledge, it is sufficient that we have good reasons for asserting the truth of that belief. Any belief whose truth we can justify by reason we can legitimately claim to constitute knowledge. This condition needs some comment. The crucial notion in it is that of "good reasons."

By this term I shall mean the following: A reason given in support of a belief or an assertion, to qualify as a good reason, must be capable of demonstrating the truth of the belief or assertion in question. It follows therefore that it is impossible for anyone to give a good reason, as I am using the term, for a belief and yet that the belief be false. If his reason for the belief is really good then it is sufficient to justify the truth of the belief. So we can vindicate moral knowledge and provide an answer to skepticism by showing that it is possible to give good reasons for believing some proposition of the form "A person has a moral obligation to perform a certain act." Since I have defined a good reason as one capable of demonstrating the truth of a proposition, an important problem that we will have to concern ourselves with is the question of what exactly constitutes a demonstration. I shall not attempt to answer that question now but will consider it further in the course of the book.

(Another point that I raise parenthetically is the possibility that my sufficient condition for knowledge should be a necessary condition as well. Certainly some philosophers would respond to this suggestion negatively. Although they would agree that, if we can demonstrate the truth of a proposition, we can legitimately assert that we know it to be true, they would add that there are many things which we can justly say we know to be true whose truth we cannot demonstrate. I do not intend to pursue this issue here but rather will simply make my own task in the book more difficult by adopting the position that, to vindicate moral knowledge, it is necessary to demonstrate the truth of a moral proposition. If I cannot discover a proposition asserting a moral obligation whose truth I can demonstrate I shall feel obliged to conclude that I have failed to find a satisfactory answer to the skeptics.)

Summing up the main point of the last two sections, it might be noted that the term "good reasons" appears in both. I have interpreted both duty and knowledge in terms of good reasons, saying that to call an act our duty is to imply that we can give no good reasons to justify our not doing it and that to hold that we know that the act is our duty is to imply that we can give good reasons for concluding that our asserting that it is so is true. This parallel usage emphasizes the fact that both morality and knowledge are concerned with justification, the first with the justification of our actions and the second with that of our beliefs.

5. PLAN OF THE BOOK

The plan of the book is quite simple. In the next four chapters I shall describe and then examine three different types of theory of moral knowledge all of which, either explicitly or implicitly, attempt to provide a justification for our beliefs about what we ought to do that can withstand the objections of the skeptics, in particular that posed by Hume's "deductive fallacy." In Chapter VI I return to one of the theories I have already discussed, for a reappraisal. Making use of the conclusions gained through my examination of these various theories, especially the strengths and weaknesses of each, I attempt in Chapter VII to develop a theory of moral knowledge capable of providing a defensible alternative to moral skepticism. In the final chapter I sketch very briefly the outlines of a general theory of the moral life.

This book is not an exhaustive study of theories of moral knowledge.

Rather, I have been quite selective, choosing to concentrate my attention mainly (although not exclusively) on British writers of the twentieth century. My reasons for doing so, other than the fact that an exhaustive historical study of the subject would not be feasible within the limits of a book of this type, are these: The writers I include have, I think, devoted more attention and thought to the problem of moral knowledge than any other major philosopher, with the possible exception of Kant. I believe that their writings contain the finest body of literature that can be found on the subject. Furthermore, although I consider earlier writers only occasionally, I do not disregard their views. Finally, a study of the best in twentieth-century writing on the problem of moral knowledge takes indirect advantage of the thought of earlier writers on the subject for the contemporary discussion is a development out of the tradition of Western moral philosophy.

CHAPTER II

DUTY AND GOODNESS

To the question "Why ought we to do certain acts?" most moral philosophers since Plato have answered "Because by doing these acts we produce something that is good." For such philosophers we have duties only because certain things have value; it is our duty to promote the good and eschew the evil. In this chapter I shall examine the appeal to goodness as a justification for moral obligation, by asking the questions, Can this appeal provide a *good* reason in support of our beliefs about what we ought to do? Can any knowledge about the goodness of anything yield us any knowledge about the reality of duty in general or of our duties in particular?

1. TYPES OF THEORY

Historically, the appeal to goodness as a justification for moral obligation has taken several different forms. The main theories can be classified in various ways but, for the purpose of answering the question of this book, perhaps the most helpful classification is a division into two general groups: (1) Theories that present different views of the nature of the relationship between goodness and duty and (2) theories that present different views of the nature of goodness itself. The most important theories within the first general group are (a) those that find a justification for duty in the goodness of the consequences of our acts and (b) those that find it in the goodness of the motives from which we act. The first type (a) is the utilitarian theories, which hold that the sole and sufficient reason why we ought to do an act is that our doing it will lead to the best consequences possible in the situation in which we find ourselves. The second type of theory (b), which is associated historically with Kant, has no special name; because the goodness of motives is often called *moral* goodness, I shall call theories of this type "moral goodness" theories. Moral goodness theories may in turn be subdivided into two classes, depending on the kind of motive that is held to provide the basis for moral action. This classification divides moral acts into those that are conscientiously motivated, that is, are motivated by the "sense of duty" (are done because the person believes that he ought to do them), on the one hand, and into those that are virtuously motivated, that is, are motivated by some morally commendable feeling like love, benevolence, or sympathy, on the other.

The second main way in which to distinguish theories that attempt to justify duty by an appeal to goodness is (2) by their conception of the nature of goodness itself. Here again two major types of theory can be distinguished. I shall call these (a) intuitionistic theories and (b) reductionistic theories. Intuitionistic theories hold that goodness is a unique, indefinable property which characterizes whatever is good. Reductionistic theories, on the other hand, hold that goodness is definable. (I use the term "reductionistic" here in a purely neutral, non-evaluative, sense; it seems to me to be the most apt descriptive term to apply as a label to these theories.) Because philosophers have defined "good" in a variety of ways, there are many kinds of reductionistic theory. Historically, probably the most important types of reductionism are metaphysical, theological, and naturalistic. Metaphysical reductionism defines "good" in metaphysical terms, an example being the idealist identification of goodness with Reality or Realization of the True Self; theological reductionism defines it in theological terms, as for example in Emil Brunner's view that the good is what God wills; naturalistic reductionism—or, as it is usually called, naturalism—defines it in empirical terms, a good example being R. B. Perry's equation of value with any object of any interest.

The division of theories according to the second principle (the nature of goodness) can be applied to both of the two kinds of theory of the relationship between goodness and duty. That is to say, it is possible to hold either an intuitionistic or a reductionistic utilitarian theory or an intuitionistic or reductionistic moral goodness theory. Historically, however, the more important distinction has been between intuitionistic and reductionistic utilitarian theories. For this reason I shall separate these two types of theory in my discussion, dealing with each in turn, but shall not concern myself with the distinction when I come to examine moral goodness theories.

The kinds of theories I have just listed cover, I believe, most of the historically important ways in which moral philosophers have attempted to provide a justification for duty by an appeal to goodness. Although my classification is not exhaustive, I think I have included the major theories; if none of these can succeed in providing a basis for moral knowledge, I doubt if any other theory of the same kind would be any more successful. I should add, too, that the theories included, considered as possible answers to the question at issue, are not all of equal importance. Some can be dealt with fairly summarily, others will require more extensive treatment. The theory that demands most detailed examination is intuitionistic utilitarianism, because, of all the theories which try to justify duty by an appeal to goodness, it stands the best chance, logically, of being successful. (In saying this, I do not mean to imply that intuitionistic utilitarianism is superior to the other kinds of theory in any way except this one.) Because intuitionistic utilitarianism is, in my opinion, the theory of moral obligation that is least vulnerable to objections and thus stands the best chance of being able to answer our question successfully, I shall devote the greater part of the chapter to an examination of it. Instead of turning directly to this topic, however, I shall take up briefly the question of whether any kind of utilitarian view, whether intuitionistic or reductionistic, can succeed as a theory of moral obligation. If no appeal to the goodness of its consequences can justify us in believing that we ought to do an act, then, of course, intuitionistic utilitarianism is ruled out *a fortiori*. The thesis that no utilitarian theory can provide an adequate explanation of our duties has been maintained by an influential group of moral philosophers in recent years—the deontologists. I shall begin, therefore, with a short discussion of their critique of utilitarianism in general.

2. THE DEONTOLOGISTS' CRITIQUE OF UTILITARIANISM

According to the utilitarian theory, to know that we ought to do a certain act in a given situation, we need only know that the act will produce better consequences than any other act we could do in that situation. Whatever act will produce the best consequences possible is always the act that we ought to do. The deontologists deny this contention, holding, on the contrary, that in some situations we ought to do a certain act even though we may know that we could in that situation have produced better consequences by doing another act instead. In support of their criticism of utilitarianism, they argue that the utilitarians distort the way in which we actually decide, in a practical moral situation, what we ought to do. To take an example, if we find ourselves faced with the decision of whether or not we ought to fulfil a promise we have made and conclude that we could producebetter consequences by breaking the promise than by keeping it, we do not, as the utilitarians contend, necessarily conclude that we ought to break it. Unless the disparity of the goodness of the consequences to be produced by the alternative acts is quite great, we believe that it is still our duty to keep the promise. Our reason for believing this is simply that we have made the promise and, as W. D. Ross remarks, "a promise is a promise."[1] This fact, rather than that of the goodness of its consequences, is what makes keeping a promise our duty. The same sort of explanation, furthermore, must be given of other types of acts, e.g., paying debts, telling the truth, righting wrongs we have committed, and so on. Because in some situations our duty cannot be determined by the goodness of the consequences of our actions, the fact that we may know that a certain act will produce the best consequences possible in a given situation does not imply that we can know that we ought to do the act. For it may be that we ought, in the situation in question, to do another act. Because this is true, utilitarianism cannot be an adequate theory of moral knowledge.

The question of whether the deontologists can sustain their case against utilitarianism is an interesting one and very difficult to answer. Fortunately, for the purpose of our argument, we do not have to decide that issue. For the deontologists do not contend that it is *never* our duty to do the act that will have the best consequences in any given situation but only that it is *not always* our duty to do so. They readily admit that, if we know that a certain act will produce the best consequences possible, *sometimes* we can know that it is our duty to do it. In their opinion, utilitarianism, although not an adequate theory of moral knowledge, is, nevertheless, not a completely mistaken one. We must simply realize that, to have an adequate theory, we must supplement the appeal to consequences in certain special situations with arguments of a non-utilitarian kind. But our question in this book is whether utilitarianism can *ever* give us any good reasons for concluding that our beliefs about what we ought to do are true and can be known to be so. Since the objections raised to utilitarianism by the deontologists do not deny the possibility of its providing us with a justification for what we ought to do in some situations, these objections cannot destroy it as a theory of moral knowledge hence cannot be used as a support for moral skepticism. If the only objections to utilitarianism were those raised by the deontologists, our problem would be much easier than in fact it is.

[1] W. D. Ross, *The Right and the Good* (Oxford, 1930), p. 35.

3. INTUITIONISTIC UTILITARIANISM AS A THEORY OF MORAL KNOWLEDGE

Intuitionistic utilitarianism begins with the assumption that certain states of affairs are intrinsically good (or intrinsically bad).[1] This assumption is not defended but is held to be self-evident, or axiomatic. We know something to be intrinsically good by means of intuition, or direct insight. When we assert that something is good, we are attributing to it the quality, intrinsic goodness. This quality is simple, indefinable, non-natural, and dependent only on the intrinsic nature of the object that possesses it. When we act our actions have consequences, sometimes good and sometimes bad. As moral beings it is always our duty to act in such a way that the consequences of our action will be the best possible—or, in a situation in which no positively good consequences can be promoted, to act in such a way that the consequences will be the least bad possible. And by the word "best" the intuitionistic utilitarians mean "possessing the greatest amount possible of the unique, intuitively apprehended quality, intrinsic goodness—or the least of its opposite, intrinsic badness." To apply this theory in a concrete moral situation is, in principle, a quite simple matter. The intuitionistic utilitarian has at his disposal a syllogistic argument that he can use to decide, on any occasion, what he ought to do (although he may and often does employ it only implicitly). This practical syllogism can be stated as follows:

State of affairs X will be the best possible consequence that can be produced by any action I can do in the present situation.

My performance of act A will produce state of affairs X.

Therefore, I ought to do act A.

Though I have stated the syllogism in a specific form, something which must be done to relate the theory to the moral decisions we actually must make, it can be stated quite generally. For the relationship between goodness and duty which it asserts is held to apply universally. Any agent, in any situation involving a moral decision, can determine what his duty is by the same method.

To evaluate intuitionistic utilitarianism as a theory of moral

---

[1] My discussion of intuitionistic utilitarianism will be based mainly on the writings of G. E. Moore, for the obvious reason that he is the most eminent representative of the position, but also because he devoted so much attention, over a long period of time, to the problem of moral knowledge, both altering and re-emphasizing, in later works, the views he had held in earlier.

knowledge what we must do is to determine whether it can ever provide us with a good reason for concluding that we know that we ought to do any action. Using the syllogism I have given as a model illustrating the relationship the theory asserts to hold between the goodness of the consequences of our actions and our duty to act, I think we have to raise the question of knowledge in at least three places: (1) In the major premise. When the major premise asserts that state of affairs X will be the best possible result attainable by any action I can do in the situation in question, this means, in intuitionistic terms, that it will possess the greatest amount possible of the unique quality, intrinsic goodness. So the question can be asked: How do we know that state of affairs X (or any state of affairs) possesses or even can possess the quality goodness—simple, indefinable, non-natural, and intrinsic? If the conclusion we reach regarding our duty is to constitute knowledge, it is necessary to establish both that we can truly attribute the quality, goodness, to certain states of affairs and that we can accurately estimate the amount of the quality present in different states of affairs. (2) In the minor premise. Even if we know that state of affairs X is the best possible consequence attainable, we cannot conclude that we know that we ought to do act A, unless we know that performance of A will produce X as its consequence. (3) In the syllogism as a whole. Finally, to know that we ought to do act A (and granting that we know both premises to be true), we must be able to show that our conclusion that we ought to do it follows from the premises. If the truth of the conclusion is to rest on the argument presented, then this argument must be formally valid.

In this chapter I shall discuss at length only question (3), because it is most directly concerned with the relationship between the goodness of the consequences of our acts and our duty to perform them, hence most directly concerned with intuitionistic utilitarianism as a theory of moral knowledge. I shall assume therefore, for purposes of the argument, that there are situations in which both premises of the syllogism can be known to be true and shall only ask: Knowing these to be true, is it possible to show that we can know the conclusion to be true as well? I need not point out that the assumption I am making is a large one. For the questions I raised under (1) and (2) are not easy to answer. The first, in particular, raises theoretical problems that, in addition to being extremely difficult, are of crucial importance to the entire theory. To justify my not dealing with this question, I hope to show that the issue of whether or not intuitionistic utilitarianism is a satisfactory theory of moral knowledge can be answered without raising it.

Question (2) is important also but more in a practical than in a theoretical way. Unless we know that a given act will in fact lead to the best consequences possible in a given situation, we cannot know that we ought to do the act. But it can be argued that we never know at the time of decision that any act will lead to the best consequences possible for at least the simple reason that any such "knowledge" would necessarily be knowledge of the future, hence would be fallible and thus not really knowledge at all. So we can never know that we ought to do any act. Because of the limitations of human knowledge no theory that bases our duty in any way on an appeal to the consequences of our acts can show that we are ever able to know, at the time when we must act, what we ought to do.

A utilitarian can meet this objection in two ways. First, he can modify the minor premise of our syllogism slightly so that instead of reading "My performance of act A will produce state of affairs X," it will read "I have good reason to believe that my performance of act A will produce state of affairs X" and then go on to specify what he means by the phrase "good reason."[1] This modification accepts the limitations on our knowledge of the future and argues, in effect, that what we morally ought to do are the acts that we believe, for very good reason, will have the best consequences possible, regardless of whether they actually do have these consequences. If this modification is accepted, the utilitarian argues, we can know what act we ought to do because we can know what act we believe with good reason will produce the best possible consequences. Secondly, the utilitarian can point out that the objection does not in principle destroy the possibility of a utilitarian justification of moral knowledge for, even if it is true that we can never know, in a specific situation, which act will produce the best possible consequences and which therefore we ought to do, we can know that there is *some* act that will do so, hence we can know that there is some act that we ought to do, even though we can never know in a given case which particular act it is.

I shall not pursue the points I have just raised any further, not because I have disposed of them, but because the main problem to be solved concerns question (3), to which I now turn. The question to be answered here may be put in this way: If we assume that we know both premises of the syllogism I have given to be true, can we legiti-

[1] Cf. G. E. Moore, *Ethics* (Oxford, 1947), pp. 118 ff.

mately assert that we know the conclusion to be true also? Can we derive a conclusion about what we ought to do from the premises that we have been given? In particular, can we do so without committing the deductive fallacy?

4. THE IDENTIFICATION OF GOODNESS AND DUTY

According to one view that has been held by intuitionistic utilitarians, to ask the questions I have just raised is to beg the question against their theory. For these questions (as well as the use of a model syllogism) assume that the utilitarians must hold that it is necessary to *deduce* our conclusions about what we ought to do from premises in which it is asserted that we can, by performing a certain act, produce consequences better than any that could be produced by the performance of any other act. Actually, however, no deduction is necessary. For the so-called conclusion is identical in meaning with the premises from which it is supposedly deduced. In his *Principia Ethica* G. E. Moore writes, "That the assertion 'I am morally bound to perform this action' is identical with the assertion 'This action will produce the greatest possible amount of good in the Universe'... is demonstrably certain"[1] and "Our 'duty' therefore, can only be defined as that action, which will cause more good to exist in the Universe than any possible alternative."[2] Now, if this view were true, it would follow that, if we granted the possibility that we could know (a) that a certain consequence X would be the best possible state of affairs attainable by any action we could do in the situation in which we are and (b) that the performance of act A would produce X, we could know (c) that we ought to do act A. For to know the truth of the conclusion is the same as to know the truth of the premises because there really is no argument from premises to conclusion at all. Rather, what I have called premises on the one hand and conclusion on the other are in fact identical with each other.

In objection to Moore's view I think we must say that it is simply not true that the assertions "I am morally bound to perform this action" and "This action will produce the greatest possible amount of

---

[1] G. E. Moore, *Principia Ethica* (Cambridge, 1903), p. 147. Although Moore later gave up this view, I think it is worth examining because, if nothing else, it is, *prima facie*, a logically possible solution to our problem within the terms of a utilitarian theory. Moore discusses the view at some length in "A Reply to My Critics," in *The Philosophy of G. E. Moore*, ed. P. Schilpp, 2d. ed. (New York, 1952). See especially pp. 358–360.

[2] Moore, *Principia Ethica*, p. 148.

good in the Universe" are identical. By "identical" Moore means "identical in meaning." For the propositions to be identical in meaning all the concepts appearing in one would have to be reducible without remainder to some concept or group of concepts appearing in the other. But this is clearly not true. For the first assertion says something about *me* (the agent) whereas the second does not mention *me* at all. If the two assertions were identical in meaning, the concept "I" would have to be identical with, or reducible to, some concept or concepts in the second. But it is not so reducible. Nor is the concept *the Universe*, that appears in the second, reducible to any concepts appearing in the first, and so on.

One other comment. If Moore's identification of the two assertions were accepted, it would follow that his appeal to the goodness of an action's consequences could never furnish a *reason* for our holding the action to be our duty. For our presumed reason would be simply a restatement of the original assertion. We should be saying "I am morally bound to do this action and the reason why I am morally bound to do it is that I am morally bound to do it." But this is no reason at all. It does not follow, of course, that the assertion of duty is unreasonable, in the sense of being untrue, simply because what seems to be a reason for it turns out, on inspection, not to be a reason. However, I think that Moore, when he made the identification in *Principia Ethica*, felt that he was giving a reason, based on the goodness of the consequences of our acts, for our beliefs about what we ought to do.

5. THE "OUGHT-TO-BE" ARGUMENT

One interesting attempt made by an intuitionistic utilitarian to show that a conclusion about what we ought to do can legitimately be drawn from the premises of his theory is that of Moore's contemporary, Hastings Rashdall. In his *The Theory of Good and Evil* Rashdall writes: "That action is right which tends to bring about the good. There is no attempt here to get rid of the ultimate unanalysable 'ought.' The good is that which 'ought' to be." In a footnote he adds, "'Good,' 'Ought' (when applied to ends), 'Value,' 'the End' I regard as synonymous terms," and, a little later, "It is implied in the idea of 'good' that it ought to be promoted..."[1] Although Rashdall does not elaborate his

---

[1] H. Rashdall, *The Theory of Good and Evil*, 2d. ed. (Oxford, 1924), I, 135, 135 n. 1, and 138. In at least one place Moore indicates a line of reasoning similar to Rashdall's. Cf. *Principia Ethica*, p. viii.

argument formally, I think it can be developed in terms similar to those I gave in the model syllogism in § 3. To accommodate his line of thought, however, we must alter the syllogism somewhat. The crux of Rashdall's argument lies in the relationship he believes to exist between "good" and "ought to be." Although he is not completely definite on the point, he seems to believe that the two can be identified. The good is that which "ought to be." We can reformulate our syllogism along the lines he is suggesting, then, by altering its major premise to read "State of affairs X ought to be" rather than "State of affairs X will be the best possible consequence..." (assuming here that "best possible consequence" can be considered equivalent to "good"). The syllogism would then read:

State of affairs X ought to be.

My performance of act A will produce state of affairs X.

Therefore, My performance of act A ought to be, or I ought to do act A.

If we grant the assumption that we know the premises of this new syllogism to be true, it would appear that we can know its conclusion to be true also. For the syllogism seems to be formally valid.

To decide whether Rashdall's argument is cogent, however, we must look more closely at its crucial link, the concept "ought to be." Just what does Rashdall mean by the notion of "ought to be," which he seems to identify with "good"? In particular, what is the relationship between the "ought" that appears in this phrase and the "ought" of moral obligation? Are the two the same or are they different? Let us examine both alternatives. Assuming, first, that the "ought" in "ought to be" is the "ought" of obligation (and also that the word "be" means "exist"), we can conclude that Rashdall, when he says that the good is "that which 'ought' to be," is implying that the good has a moral obligation to exist. But can this be? The good in question, which in Rashdall's argument provides the final justification for our having a duty to act, must either exist or not exist. If it does exist it cannot furnish any basis for a duty because our reason for concluding that act A is our duty is that its performance will produce or bring into existence state of affairs X (which is the good in this case). If X already exists it would be meaningless to say we ought to bring it into existence. For us to have any duty to act, clearly the good or that which "ought to be" must not yet be. If the "ought" in "ought to be" is the "ought" of moral obligation, we are forced to conclude that a non-existent good has an obligation to exist. But this is impossible; for we cannot meaningfully attribute a moral obligation to something that does not exist.

If we assume that Rashdall did mean his "ought to be" to embody a moral "ought"—as he seems to do—then I think we can fairly say that he was led astray because he failed to examine carefully enough the fairly common locution "ought to be." Had he done so he would have realized that it is one of the many quite loose expressions in common use that can be interpreted in such a way that they are meaningful but which, when taken literally, are nonsense. For example, when some of us during the last war said, "There ought to be peace in the world," I think what we meant was "It would be good if there were peace" or "I wish for peace" or "Those in power ought to end the war" or something of that sort. What we never, by any stretch of the imagination, meant was, "Peace has a moral obligation to appear in the world." But it is just this absurdity that must be applied to "good" to make Rashdall's deduction work.

But let us look at the other alternative—that in the phrase "ought to be" Rashdall does not mean the "ought" to be the "ought" of moral obligation. In this case we might well ask just what he does mean by the "ought." However, we need not pursue the point because his acceptance of this alternative would immediately destroy his case. As a glance at the syllogism will quickly show, he is now left with an attempted deduction which is formally invalid. For its conclusion contains the concept "ought" (in the sense of moral obligation) but its premises, although they contain the word "ought" do not contain the concept of moral obligation. The argument thus falls victim to the deductive fallacy.

6. THE DEDUCTIVE ARGUMENT—A RESTATEMENT

By far the most carefully and completely worked-out attempt to provide a justification for duty on intuitionistic utilitarian terms appears in G. E. Moore's last major writing "A Reply to My Critics." In it Moore criticizes sharply some of his own earlier views on the subject and then proceeds to state a new position, which he develops in a series of different and increasingly complex formulations. Moore is not directly concerned in the argument in question with the problem of showing how moral knowledge is possible but rather with making clear the precise relationship between propositions about intrinsic goodness and propositions about moral obligation. However, if the conclusion he reaches about this relationship is correct and if we assume, as we have for the purposes of argument done, that propositions about goodness can be known to be true, it will follow that propositions about moral obligation can be known to be true as well; hence Moore's theory will provide a satisfactory answer to the question of how moral knowledge is possible.

Moore states his view at least four different times, in slightly different ways, the final formulation being the most elaborate and complex.[1] Since the complexities of his statement result mainly from his attempt to make his position as precise as he possibly can and to avoid certain criticisms raised against his earlier views, reasons that do not affect the problem with which we are concerned, instead of using his formulation I shall state the issue in quite simple terms. Though this statement would be inadequate for some purposes—a detailed critical analysis of Moore's ethics, for example—I think that it will be adequate for ours. Such a simplification, besides, will allow us more readily to concentrate our attention on the problem at hand and to avoid getting bogged down in side-issues. The question may be put in this way: What is the relationship between propositions or, as Moore more precisely puts it, propositional functions of the form (1) "X is intrinsically good" and (2) "We have a duty to do action A, which will produce X"? Moore rejects the view that he had held in *Principia Ethica* (which I have criticized in § 4) that the two propositions are identical in meaning. His reason for doing so is that we can think the first, that something is intrinsically good, without thinking the second, that we have a duty to perform the act that will produce it. If the two were identical, thinking the one would be the same as thinking the other. To clarify the distinction he is making Moore uses an analogy which becomes very important later in his argument. Consider the two propositions: "X is a cube" and "X has twelve edges." These are not identical in meaning for we can think the one without thinking the other. Moreover, as he implies, most of us recognize cubes long before we are aware that such

---

[1] See Moore, "A Reply to My Critics," *op. cit.*, pp. 560–563, 571–577, 598–601, and 606–611. These formulations occur within the context of Moore's reply to criticisms raised against his theories by W. K. Frankena, in his essay "Obligation and Value in the Ethics of G. E. Moore" (pp. 93–110). It is somewhat difficult to extricate Moore's final view on the question we are considering from this context; however, I think that Moore does develop a quite definite position in the passages I have noted, which reveals itself on careful reading.

objects do have twelve edges.[1] Analogously, Moore contends, the same thing is true of the two propositions, (1) and (2), about intrinsic goodness and duty. Moore's argument here is psychological, being based on what is "before our minds" when we think certain things, and could be criticized, possibly to some effect, on the grounds that the nature of our psychological awareness is irrelevant to the meaning of propositions. Nevertheless, whether his argument is acceptable or not, I believe his conclusion is correct; in neither case are the two propositions identical in meaning. But if (1) and (2)—the propositions about goodness and duty, respectively—are not identical, how are they related? Moore's answer is that they are *logically equivalent* to each other. By this he means that each follows logically from the other. To assert (1) and deny (2) or to assert (2) and deny (1) would be self-contradictory. In support of this conclusion Moore makes use of the analogy already mentioned, arguing that the logical relationship between propositions (1) and (2) is the same as that between "X is a cube" and "X is a cube and has twelve edges." Just as the statement "X is a cube but does not have twelve edges" is self-contradictory so the statement "X is intrinsically good but we do not have a duty to do action A, which will produce X" is self-contradictory as well.[2] Applying this conclusion to our problem, if we assume that we can know that a proposition of the form "X is intrinsically good" is true, we can conclude that we can know that a proposition of the form "We have a duty to do action A, which will produce X" is true also. For to assert the former and to deny the latter would be self-contradictory. Therefore we can conclude that intuitionistic utilitarianism provides us with a justification for moral knowledge.

The cogency of Moore's argument rests on the question of whether or not propositions (1) and (2) are logically equivalent. What reasons does Moore have for believing that they are? The only reason that he gives in his essay is that these two propositions are analogous, in this vital respect, to the two propositions concerning a cube. His argument might be put in this way: If the propositions concerning the cube are logically equivalent, then the propositions about goodness and duty are logically equivalent as well. We know that those about the cube are so, therefore we can conclude that those about goodness and duty are so too.

Moore's argument can be attacked at two points at least. For one thing, it might be questioned whether the propositions about the cube

[1] Cf. *ibid.*, p. 599.
[2] Cf. *ibid.*, esp. pp. 598–601 and 606–608.

really are logically equivalent and, for another, whether the propositions about goodness and duty are analogous to those about the cube in the way required by the argument. I believe that Moore could answer any attack on the first point by demonstrating that the cube propositions *are* logically equivalent. However, I do not see how he could successfully meet an attack on the second point. For the one argument that can show the logical equivalence of the cube propositions cannot be applied to the propositions about goodness and duty. Thus the analogy on which he rests his case is a faulty one. The faultiness of his analogy becomes clear as soon as we analyze the two sets of propositions in question. If "X is a cube but it does not have twelve edges" is self-contradictory, then "X has twelve edges" follows logically from "X is a cube."[1] But how do we know that the original proposition is self-contradictory? I think that the answer must be that we can *deduce* the proposition "X has twelve edges" from "X is a cube." Given the definition of cube, it follows necessarily, by the deductive rules of mathematics, that X *must* have twelve edges. If an object does not have twelve edges, it is logically impossible for it to be a cube. And this impossibility can be demonstrated.

Now what about the analogy between the twelve-edged cube and the good that ought to be promoted? If the analogy is sound, it must be possible, I am contending, to deduce some proposition of the form "We ought to do action A, which will produce X" from a proposition of the form "X is intrinsically good." Now Moore, in his presentation, never gives any hint as to how such a deduction might be carried out. All that he does is to affirm that the second proposition follows logically from the first.[2] Then, for his only reason for affirming that it does, he asserts that the relationship is analogous to that of the cube and its edges. But the relationship surely is not analogous. For, whatever one can deduce from the definition of a cube, from an assertion about intrinsic goodness one cannot deduce anything about what we ought to do. Any attempt to do so results in the commission of the deductive fallacy. The attempted deduction is necessarily formally invalid because its conclusion contains a concept that does not appear in the

---

[1] However, the proposition "X has twelve edges but is not a cube" is not self-contradictory hence the proposition "X is a cube" does not follow logically from "X has twelve edges." The *logically equivalent* propositions are, rather, "X is a cube" and "X is a cube and has twelve edges." Cf. *ibid.*, p. 599.

[2] He contends that the first follows logically from the second as well (i.e., that the two are logically equivalent) but, since this relationship does not affect our problem, I shall disregard it.

premises. Had Moore carefully analyzed the analogy he assumed to hold between the relationship that a cube has to twelve edges and that goodness has to duty, rather than simply asserting it, he would, I believe, have been forced to conclude that it does not hold. Because it does not hold, we have to conclude that Moore's final theory, that the propositions "We have a duty to do action A, which will produce X" and "X is intrinsically good" are logically equivalent to each other, breaks down. Therefore, even though we may know that some proposition about intrinsic goodness is true, such knowledge does not give us the reason Moore thought it did for concluding that we know any proposition about our duty to be true.

7. THE APPEAL TO SELF-EVIDENCE

The three theories that I have just examined (in §'s 4–6) have one important feature in common; they all hold that there is some kind of logical relationship between the goodness of the consequences of our acts and our duty to perform the acts, which is capable of making it possible for us to know that we have a moral obligation to do these acts. In *Principia Ethica* Moore argued that the notions of utilitarian goodness and duty are identical and in "A Reply to My Critics" he held them to be logically equivalent. Rashdall, on the other hand, attempted to deduce the notion of "ought" from that of "good" by introducing the intermediary notion "ought to be." All of these theories, I think, fail.

If the utilitarians rested their belief in the reality of duty simply on these arguments, I think we should have to conclude that utilitarianism offers no hope of providing a satisfactory theory of moral knowledge. As a matter of fact, however, they do not—at least, not completely. For one can find in the writings of Moore and Rashdall (as well as other moral philosophers of their persuasion) a quite different approach to the issue. This approach is intuitionistic, rather than logical. Indeed, it compounds intuitions. It agrees with the theories I have already discussed in holding that certain propositions of the form "X is intrinsically good" are self-evident and their truth recognized by direct intuitive insight. In addition, moreover, it holds that the proposition "It is always our duty to do the act that will produce the best possible consequences in the situation in which we find ourselves" is self-evident and intuitively known to be so. By appealing to intuitive self-evidence to justify our duty to act in the way that will promote the best possible consequences, it avoids the objections that I have raised against the theories that attempt to find some kind of logical connection between goodness and duty. For it gives up the attempt to derive our duties from the notion of goodness by logical means. Goodness and duty, it holds, are not identical in meaning, they are not logically equivalent to each other, nor is it possible to deduce the latter from the former. Nevertheless the two are necessarily related to each other in such a way that, if X is the best possible consequence of any act we can perform in the situation in which we find ourselves and our performance of act A will produce X, then it is our duty to do act A. Although no argument will prove that this relationship holds, we know that it does because we directly apprehend it to be so. Assuming that we know that certain states of affairs are intrinsically good, the intuitionistic utilitarians believe we can know that certain acts are our duties. Thus, moral knowledge is possible.

I shall not here attempt to examine the specific question of the self-evidence of the utilitarian thesis that it is always our duty to do the act that will produce the best possible consequences in the situation in which we find ourselves. As I have already remarked (in § 2) moral philosophers like the deontologists, who themselves appeal to intuition as the basis for moral knowledge, have denied this utilitarian claim to be self-evident. To discuss the controversy between the utilitarians and the deontologists in detail would require too long a digression from the main theme of this book. Rather than taking this point up specifically, I shall limit myself to an examination of the general issue of whether the appeal to intuitive self-evidence—whether made by a utilitarian, a deontologist, or anyone else—can provide a justification for our beliefs about what we ought to do capable of withstanding the attacks of the skeptics. I shall postpone this task until Chapter VI.

8. REDUCTIONISTIC UTILITARIANISM

At the beginning of the chapter I divided utilitarian theories of moral obligation into two kinds—intuitionistic and reductionistic—the former holding that the concept of goodness is unique and indefinable, the latter defining it in a variety of ways, the type of definition given determining the kind of reductionistic theory resulting, for example, theological reductionism, naturalism, and so on. I went on to say that intuitionistic utilitarianism is superior to any form of reductionistic utilitarianism in its ability to provide a theoretical justification for moral obligation. My reason for this judgment is the following: Utilitarianism, whether intuitionistic or reductionistic, attempts to justify our belief that we have duties through an appeal to the goodness of the consequences of our acts. The concept of goodness, thus, enters into both types of theory, the difference between the two being that intuitionistic utilitarianism takes this concept to be unique and indefinable whereas reductionistic utilitarian theories attempt to define it in terms of something else. Both types of theory, considered simply as theories of moral obligation, hence, are subject to criticism on the same point, namely, whether the relationship between goodness and duty which they assert to hold really does hold. Reductionistic utilitarian theories, however, can be attacked on still another point, namely, whether the definitions that they give of the notion of goodness are acceptable. The importance of this second point of attack need hardly be emphasized; it is sufficient to remark that Moore's "naturalistic fallacy" is an attempt to demonstrate that no definitions of goodness can ever be successful. The difficulty of determining whether the "naturalistic fallacy" really is a fallacy or not is well attested by the fact that the problem has been assiduously discussed pro and con for over half a century without a firm conclusion yet having been reached. To realize this all that one need do is pick up the most recent book written by a naturalist, where he will find it asserted that Moore's arguments have all been disposed of, and then turn to one written by a non-naturalist, where he will read that naturalism has been conclusively refuted.

I do not plan to discuss the "naturalistic fallacy" in detail in this book (although I shall probably refer to it briefly from time to time), my reason being that I think the solution to the problem I am concerned with does not turn on the question of whether the attempt to define goodness constitutes a fallacy. I believe that the logical relationship between intuitionistic utilitarianism and all varieties of reductionistic utilitarianism, considered as theories of moral obligation, is such that the former could be true even though none of the latter was but that, if it is not true, then none of them can be. Therefore, to the extent that the criticisms of intuitionistic utilitarianism I have made in this chapter are cogent, they will hold *a fortiori* against all forms of reductionistic utilitarianism.

There are several objections that a reductionist might make to my conclusion. I shall try to answer the two that seem to me most important. First, it might be argued that I have misconstrued the logic of the reductionistic theories of obligation by implying that, in order to justify our beliefs about what we ought to do, they must employ an argument involving two distinct steps; (1) the definition of goodness in terms of some notion such as the will of God or "any object of any interest" and (2) the derivation of our obligations from the concept of goodness so defined. On the contrary, what these theories really do is to eliminate the concept of goodness from the argument completely, replacing it with the notions I have just referred to as definitions of goodness (or others like them), and then argue directly from these notions to conclusions about moral obligation. So my arguments against intuitionistic utilitarianism, which all rested on the impossibility of deriving our duties from the concept of goodness, miss them altogether.

Whether or not reductionistic utilitarians *might* state their theories in the way I have just suggested and escape the objections I have raised in this chapter, the fact remains that they have not actually done so. On the contrary, most reductionists make a great point of the fact that they are offering a definition of "good." Early in the chapter I mentioned the definitions given by Perry and Brunner. It is hardly necessary to remind anyone of Mill's famous equation of the "desirable" with the "desired." This list could be added to almost indefinitely. Why are the reductionists so concerned with giving a definition of "good"? Whether they make the point explicitly or not, I think it is clear that the reason is this: They accept the utilitarian thesis that our duties must be justified by an appeal to the *goodness* of the consequences of our acts. Having made this assumption, they then go on to define goodness—as that which God wills, as an object of an interest, and so on. If this analysis of the logic of reductionistic utilitarian thinking is correct, then any refutation of intuitionistic utilitarianism as a theory of moral obligation will be *a fortiori* a refutation of reductionistic utilitarianism. For, if "good" can be defined in other terms, then its meaning is identical with that in terms of which it has been defined. It follows, therefore, that, if it is impossible satisfactorily to justify our duties by an appeal to goodness, it will be impossible to do so by an appeal to any concept which is held to be identical in meaning with goodness.

But let us assume, for the sake of argument, that a reductionist should eliminate all reference to the notion of goodness from his theory and argue that he derives his conclusions about what we ought to do directly from certain assertions about, say, the will of God, or our desires, or the objects that interest us. Could he, by doing this, succeed in producing a satisfactory theory of moral obligation? I think not. For he would, inevitably and obviously, run afoul of the deductive fallacy. The attempt to provide a justification for our duties in any such terms, to be successful, would of necessity somewhere have to deduce an "ought" from an "is." And this is logically impossible.

The second objection to my conclusion is one that would be raised only by naturalists. Some naturalists might say that, besides distorting their view in the way just mentioned, I have distorted it in quite another way by my assumption that a justification of moral obligation must take some logically deductive form. Rather than using deductive logic, they would maintain, what we must do is to adopt the methodology of the empirical sciences and employ an inductive argument. Put very briefly and sketchily, the job of moral philosophers, as these writers see it, is to find out, by such techniques as interviews, the observation of behavior, and the compilation of statistics, just what people do think to be good, what they think to be their duty, and how they reason from their views concerning goodness to the decisions they make about what they ought to do. If we gather enough data and are able to employ a sufficiently precise scientific method, we can, by inductive generalization, come to certain limited conclusions about moral obligation. These conclusions will never be final or absolute but they are capable in principle of attaining a knowledge-status approaching that of the physical sciences. And this is certainly all we can or need ask of them.

The first observation to be made concerning this argument is that any conclusion about moral obligation that a naturalist could reach by employing the method indicated would take the form of a statement about what someone (or some group) thought to be his duties—or, possibly, a statement about the observed behavior of people acting in the belief that certain acts were their duties. But the problem we are concerned with is the question: How can we know what our duties *really are* or that we *do have* duties? The conclusions reached by the naturalist could answer our question only if it could be shown that the beliefs regarding their duties held by the people he has observed are *true*. But this no empirical survey of people's beliefs can ever determine. To state the point in another way, the procedure that I have described and attributed to some naturalists is not philosophical at all but rather scientific. To say this, of course, is neither to condemn it nor to belittle it but simply to distinguish it from philosophy, adding that conclusions reached by its methods can never give an answer to a philosophical question. But the question we are trying to answer is a philosophical one.

With this distinction at least some naturalists would agree. But they would then go on to add that the philosophical question of how moral knowledge is possible cannot be answered. So we had better forget about it and devote our energies to questions that can be answered as, for example, questions about what people take to be their duties and questions concerning the various causal relationships between people's beliefs on this subject and such things as their economic and social status, early upbringing, religious convictions, and so on. In other words, we should give up being moral philosophers and become social scientists. But, if we accept this alternative for the reason given (as many naturalists have done), we have joined the ranks of the moral skeptics. For we have admitted that moral knowledge is impossible.

Before ending this section I should like to add a brief comment. Although I believe that no form of reductionistic *utili*tarianism can provide an acceptable theory of moral obligation, I do not think that the reductionistic approach to morality should be completely abandoned. Rather it seems to me that much of what the naturalists maintain can be formulated in a way that is both plausible and defensible. What naturalism cannot give is, as I have already argued, a satisfactory justification for the reality of duty. But it may be possible to formulate a satisfactory moral theory basically naturalistic in character, but supplemented in a way that will overcome the deficiencies of the usual forms of naturalism. I will not pursue this suggestion further here but will return to it later.

9. MORAL GOODNESS AND DUTY

In § 1 of this chapter I divided theories that attempt to justify duty by an appeal to goodness into two types, which I called, respectively, utilitarian theories and moral goodness theories. I have discussed utilitarianism and shall turn now, briefly, to examine moral goodness theories. Theories of this type contend that we can justify our belief that we have a duty to do certain acts by an appeal to the goodness of the acts themselves. The acts are good not because of what is done but because of the motive from which it is done. Motives which can render acts morally good are (1) "the sense of duty," which gives rise to conscientious acts, or (2) some good desire or feeling such as love or pity or benevolence, which gives rise to virtuous acts. To decide whether moral goodness theories can solve the problem of moral knowledge, we must decide whether the fact that an action, if done, will be either conscientiously or virtuously motivated gives us a good reason for concluding that we ought to do it. If we can answer this question affirmatively, then we can know that we ought to do any given act, if we can show that we know that, if we do this act, we will be motivated to do so either by the sense of duty or by some virtuous feeling like pity or love. The first question is the crucial one: Can the fact that, if we do an act, we shall do it from either a conscientious or a virtuous motive ever give us any reason for believing that we ought to do it?

I begin with virtuous acts. Suppose a person, motivated by love or pity, comes to the aid of a stranger in distress. Let us assume, for purposes of argument, that, in the case in question, it was this person's duty to help the stranger. His action, because of its virtuous motive, was morally good. The action was also, by hypothesis, his duty. Can the second fact, that the act was his duty, be derived in any way from the first fact, that, because of its motive, it was morally good? The moral goodness in question, being the goodness of the man's action and resulting from the motive from which he has acted, comes into existence only with his performance of the act. Thus there is no moral goodness in the situation until he has acted. But this goodness, to be able to render the act his duty *before* it is performed, obviously must itself exist before the act is performed. Since the goodness does not exist before the act, the act cannot be his duty before it has been done; it becomes his duty only after he has done it. But *then* it cannot be his duty *to do the act* because he has already done it. Therefore, if this theory of obligation were correct, no one could ever have a duty to do any act at all.

However, it might be argued that, even though we could not, on this theory, ever have any duties, it might still be possible for us to conclude about a past action that it *was* our duty (because we had acted virtuously in doing it) or of a possible action that it *would be* our duty (if we were to act virtuously in doing it). We can eliminate the second alternative, about a possible action that it would be our duty if we were to act virtuously in doing it, because our problem is whether we can provide good reasons for concluding that we know that we ought to do anything; and the knowledge that the possible act would be our duty cannot become knowledge that it really is our duty until the condition stated in the "if" clause is fulfilled, in other words, until we perform the act virtuously. But this puts us in the same impossible position that we were in before. There remains the first alternative— that we can know of acts that we have done that they were our duties. No act is our duty before we do it but can become our duty (or "the act that was our duty") only after we have done it. I have serious doubts as to whether this theory is even meaningful. For the notion "act that was our duty" here does not mean "act that was our duty before we performed it, sometime in the past" but rather "act that was performed sometime in the past, and became our duty after we performed it." And this last characterization is nonsensical. Furthermore, even if the theory were meaningful, it would be of academic interest only. It could never give us any help in solving our practical moral problems. For what we want to know is what we ought to do *now*, what our duty in *this* situation is. To these queries the theory could respond only that we have no duties now.

The theory that an act can be rendered our duty by being virtuously motivated is subject to still another criticism. This criticism rests on the fact that a virtuous act is, by definition, an act motivated by a desire. When we act virtuously, even though the specific motive leading us to act is exemplary—love of our fellow-men, say—we are doing what we want to do because we want to do it. Although the act we do may be one that we ought to do, it cannot be made so by the fact that we do it because we have a desire to do it. If this were not so, any act that we did because we wanted to do it would by that fact be made our duty. The result would be to deprive the notion of duty of any meaning. For it makes no sense to say "I have a moral obligation to do this act and the *reason* why I have the obligation is that I want to do the act." For moral obligation to have any meaning, what we ought to do must be independent of what we want to do. It is for this reason that Kant rightly concluded that the notion of obligation is not applicable to God. Because he is a perfect being he has no duties; what he wants to do is always what he "ought" to do (hence the "ought" becomes superfluous). For men, however, the "ought" is not superfluous. It is pertinent just because, unlike God, we do not always want to do what we ought to do.

Turning from virtuous to conscientious acts, it is clear that the attempt to derive our duty to perform such acts from the goodness of our motive in doing so leads us to the same paradoxical conclusion that we reached in our discussion of virtuous acts, namely, that no act can ever be our duty until after we have done it. Like the other theory, too, it is subject to a second criticism. However, in its case the criticism is somewhat different. A conscientious act is one motivated by the "sense of duty" and its moral goodness is a result of this motive. But what is the "sense of duty"? What does it mean to say that someone is motivated to act by the "sense of duty"? When we use this expression what we mean is that the person's reason for doing the act is his conviction that the act is his duty or that he ought to do the act. If this conviction is his motive for doing the act, then he has acted conscientiously and his act is morally good. Can we derive the fact that he ought to do the act from the fact that his doing it from this motive is morally good? Fairly obviously, we cannot. For his belief that he ought to do the act is either true or false. In either case, if he does the act because he believes he ought, his act will be morally good, because conscientiously motivated. However, if his belief is false we cannot derive his duty to do the act from the goodness of his motive in acting for the simple reason that the act is *not* his duty. But what if his belief is true? This means that the act really is his duty but it implies also that the act is his duty (the act he ought to do) before he ever does it. For, if his belief that he ought to do the act is his motive for doing it, this belief must exist *before* he does it. And, if the belief is true, it follows that the act really is his duty when he believes it to be, that is, before he has done it. But if the act is his duty before he ever does it, it is impossible to derive the conclusion that it is rendered his duty by the moral goodness displayed in his doing it.

In addition to these specific defects, moral goodness theories share one common shortcoming. Whether they attempt to justify our duty to act by an appeal to the goodness of a virtuous *or* a conscientious motive, they commit the deductive fallacy. To make their case they must be able to answer the question: Why do we have a duty to act from good motives? Any argument intended to produce an answer to this question will suffer, like the equivalent utilitarian argument, either by being a *non sequitur* (because it contains the notion of "ought" in its conclusion but not in its premises) or by leading into an infinite regress (each new argument containing an unjustified "ought" in its premises). For this reason, and the others I have already given, I conclude that we cannot provide a justification for moral obligation by an appeal to moral goodness, whether this be the moral goodness either of conscientious or of virtuous acts.

10. DUTY AND GOODNESS AND THE "OUGHT" AND THE "IS"

The main general conclusion that can be drawn from the argument of this chapter, I believe, is that David Hume laid bare the point of vulnerability in traditional theories of moral obligation. For all of the theories attempting to derive our duties from the concept of goodness that I have examined in the chapter either commit the deductive fallacy directly or, in attempting to avoid it, run into other insuperable difficulties, or both.

This is fairly obvious with some types of "goodness" theory, naturalistic reductionism, for example. When a naturalist concludes that we ought to do some act and, asked for a reason why we ought, replies that our doing it will satisfy someone's desires or will promote social integration, it is plain that there is a logical gap in his argument that cannot be bridged. For he can never, in terms of his own theory, provide any logically cogent reason why we ought to satisfy anyone's desires or promote social integration. What is true of naturalism, furthermore, is true of all of the theories that try to justify our duties by an appeal to goodness. The only difference is that, because some of these theories are more subtle than naturalism, the gap in their argument is not so apparent.

Not everyone would agree with me on this point. Before leaving the "goodness" theories I would like to discuss, briefly, an objection that I think Moore might make against my conclusion. Although he would probably agree that my arguments are conclusive as far as reductionistic theories are concerned, he would, I think, argue that they can be circumvented by an intuitionistic theory. He would begin by pointing out that my criticisms assume that, when it is asserted of something that it *is*, the assertion implies that the thing in question *exists*. Thus, when I maintain that the attempt to derive an "ought" from an "is" commits the deductive fallacy, the "is" that I am here referring to is the "is" of existence. And the fallaciousness of the whole attempt rests on the fact that no premises about what exists are capable of yielding conclusions about what anyone ought to do. But if anything can *be*, and nevertheless not *exist*, my argument can be evaded. This, I believe, Moore would hold to be true of goodness, as he conceives it.[1]

When we say of something that it is good we seem to be making an assertion that is in some way different from one in which we say of

---

[1] Cf. Moore, *Principia Ethica*, pp. 110–111.

something that it is red or soft. Although the term "is" appears in both statements, it seems to mean something different in each. In the second, most philosophers would agree, the "is" makes an assertion of existence, the redness or softness exists. But in the first Moore (and many other philosophers) would contend that it does not; goodness does not exist. Rather, as some philosophers like to say, it "subsists."

If we grant the distinction just made, what follows? Does it provide sufficient reason for exempting intuitionistic utilitarianism from the criticisms I have made? I think we must agree that Moore has a point in distinguishing the type of assertions of which "This is good" is an example from the type of which "This is red" is an example. Furthermore, his distinction has some relevance to our problem. Though we may agree that no conclusion about our duty can ever be deduced from premises that contain nothing but descriptive predicates, we may feel that the problem is significantly altered, and lessened, if the premises from which we argue make assertions about goodness. For goodness is not a descriptive predicate; it is a value predicate. We are not, in appealing to it, trying to deduce our obligation from a mere recital of facts; rather we are in the ethical realm already. For we are deriving our duty from premises which assert values.

All this may be true but I do not think it is sufficient to solve our problem. Certainly statements about goodness are in some important senses different from statements about redness. I would agree with Moore, further, that they are in some sense more closely related to conclusions about what we ought to do. This concession is simply another way of putting the point I made earlier in the chapter, that intuitionistic utilitarianism stands a better chance of providing an adequate basis for moral obligation than does reductionistic utilitarianism. The crucial question, however, still remains: Does intuitionistic utilitarianism succeed in providing such a basis? My answer is that it does not. For all the arguments by which it attempts to provide this basis are, as I have tried to show in this chapter, logically faulty. And this fault in them, which is logical, is not overcome by the fact, if it be one, that goodness does not exist, but only subsists. For the fatal gap in the deduction lies in the fact that the "ought" asserted in the conclusion does not appear in the premises, rather than in the fact that the goodness asserted in the premises is held either to exist or to subsist.

The conclusion to which we seem driven by the argument of this chapter is that the attempts made by philosophers to justify our duties by an appeal to goodness, whether it be the goodness of motives or of consequences, have not been successful. For all the arguments they have given in support of their positions have broken down. Unless it can be shown that there is an intuitively self-evident connection between the goodness of some state of affairs and our duty to act in a certain way, or unless an entirely new approach to the issue be found, it would certainly appear that no knowledge about goodness (should such be possible) can yield us any knowledge about how we ought to act. The conclusions of this chapter thus serve only to strengthen the case of the moral skeptics.

CHAPTER III

DUTY AND RIGHTNESS

In the last chapter (2.2) I discussed briefly the criticisms made by the deontologists against utilitarian theories of moral obligation. Although the deontologists are probably best known as critics of utilitarianism, they have also developed a theory of obligation of their own. In this chapter I shall examine that theory in the attempt to determine whether it can provide a satisfactory answer to the question of how moral knowledge is possible.

1. THE INTUITIONISM OF THE DEONTOLOGISTS

The deontologists' moral theory, as stated particularly by H. A. Prichard and W. D. Ross, is the most recent expression of a perennial point of view in moral thinking, the conviction that moral philosophy should be concerned primarily with action itself rather than with the ends to be achieved by action. According to this tradition the important moral concepts are not good and bad, but right and wrong. Although this way of thinking is associated historically with the Hebraic-Christian strand in Western thought, it was not entirely absent from Greek philosophy, being found particularly in the writings of the Stoics. In modern times it had its greatest vogue during the eighteenth century, with Kant in Germany and people like Bishop Butler and Richard Price in England. Traditionally it has come to be called "intuitionism."

As a title identifying the deontological tradition—and the contemporary deontological movement in particular—the term "intuitionism" is unfortunate, because it is used in another sense to characterize views to which the deontologists are opposed. For example, in the last chapter I used the term *intuitionistic* utilitarianism as a label for the views of Moore and Rashdall, which have been the target of much of the deontologists' criticism. Clearly the term "intuitionism" is being used in different ways when it is applied first to utilitarians and then to the deontologists because of their rejection of utilitarianism. To avoid possible confusion I shall distinguish these two uses as follows: As I used the term in the last chapter, intuitionism means a theory which holds that moral truths can be apprehended by means of direct intuition or moral insight. Such truths are for it self-evident. As the term has often been used historically, however—and this is the second use—it means a theory which holds that rightness, duty, or "oughtness" are fundamental, irreducible moral concepts, of at least equal importance to moral philosophy as the concept of goodness. This kind of intuitionism, particularly in the form in which it is held by the deontologists, denies that we can find a satisfactory basis for our duties by an appeal to the goodness either of the consequences of our actions or of our motives in acting.

Having distinguished the two meanings of the term "intuitionism," I should add that the deontologists are intuitionists in both senses of the term. For they believe not only that the notions I have just mentioned are fundamental and non-derivative but also that truths embodying them are apprehended by means of direct intuition or moral insight. In this chapter I shall be concerned with the deontologists as representatives of intuitionism, in both senses of that term. This will not, I hope, cause confusion because I think that the sense in which I am using the term "intuitionism" will be clear from the context in which it appears.

In their formulation of the intuitionistic position the deontologists have improved on the theories of earlier intuitionists in at least three important ways: (1) They have drawn much more careful distinctions among the meanings of the principal concepts of moral theory, in particular, "right," "duty," "good," and "morally good." However, as I shall argue later, they have failed to make clearly enough a distinction of considerable importance to their own theory. (2) They have avoided the extreme position that denies that the goodness of the consequences of our actions has any relevance in determining their rightness, holding instead that one of the reasons making an act our duty is the fact that its performance would result in the best possible consequences. (3) They have avoided the problem raised by the "conflict of duties," which had forced most traditional intuitionistic theories to accept the paradoxical consequence that two incompatible actions could both be our unconditional duty, by making a distinction between what Ross calls *prima facie* duties and actuel duties. For these reasons, the deontological theory is probably the best statement of the intuitionistic position that has so far been made.

Intuitionistic moral philosophers (in the second sense of the term "intuitionistic") have generally believed moral knowledge to be possible. (If they have been intuitionists in the first sense of the term also, as most of them have, they have necessarily believed in the possibility of moral knowledge.) Indeed, their theories represent one of the major historical attempts to answer the question of how we gain knowledge about what we ought to do. My object here will be to examine the answer given by the intuitionists to this question, in the form in which it has been developed in the twentieth century by the deontologists. To do this I shall have to extrapolate on one point from the views which they have explicitly formulated. Because, in the writings in which they first developed their position, the deontologists operated on the assumption that the notions of rightness and duty are synonymous, they never examined the nature of the relationship between the rightness of an act and our duty to do it. Later, when they came to question the synonymity of the two concepts, they did not follow out the implications of this questioning. Because the issue raises important theoretical problems, it should be examined. I shall take it up briefly at the end of the chapter, after I have completed my review of the theory explicitly held by the deontologists. This theory—Prichard would probably not wish to call it a theory at all—is found in the writings of both Prichard and Ross, the most concise and forceful statement of it appearing in Prichard's article (which marks the beginning of the deontological movement) "Does Moral Philosophy Rest on a Mistake?"[1] In my examination of the theory I shall use this article as a main basis for the argument.

2. PRICHARD'S "UNREASONABLE" THEORY

The title of Prichard's article is rhetorical. Of course moral philosophy rests on a mistake. In the article Prichard advances the thesis that almost all of the moral philosophers from Plato to the present, in spite of the great divergences among their theories, have one thing in common—they all commit the mistake of elaborating moral theories. To state his point less enigmatically, they assume that it is necessary to offer arguments which *prove* that we have duties or that a given act is our duty. They then develop various theories which they believe will provide the needed proof or, in other words, will furnish us with good

---

[1] H. A. Prichard, "Does Moral Philosophy Rest on a Mistake?" *Mind*, New Series—XXI (1912), 21–37.

reasons for concluding that our beliefs about our duties are true. It is Prichard's contention that such reasons neither can nor need be given. Hence all the moral theories that try to provide them, besides being fallacious, are really superfluous. The first requisite of a satisfactory moral philosophy, therefore, will be its abandonment of the attempt to elaborate a "theory" of moral knowledge. Prichard does not, however, conclude from this that our beliefs about our duties cannot be justified and thus that moral knowledge is impossible. On the contrary, the reason why these beliefs need no theoretical justification is that they are self-justifying. That certain acts are our duties is self-evident. We apprehend this fact directly by what Prichard calls an act of "*moral* thinking."[1] Such an apprehension is a case of knowledge. When we directly apprehend that a certain act is our duty in a given situation, we *know* it is our duty. The only reason for saying that we know it— and this is not a reason in the sense of a theoretical justification for our knowledge of it but rather the way in which we know it—is that we do apprehend it to be our duty.

But what if we do not know that a certain act is our duty? What if we think it is but are not sure? Or what if we come to doubt that a certain type of action that we have always thought to be our duty really is our duty? It is from doubts like these, Prichard believes, that moral philosophy has sprung. People, having come to doubt that traditionally accepted moral codes ought to be followed, began to search for reasons which would either justify acceptance of these codes or give reasons for abandoning them. The final result has been the great systems of moral philosophy that we now have. Because it is based on a false assumption, this search is essentially misguided and the moral theories that have resulted a great mistake. For if we come to doubt that we ought to perform a certain act, we can never be given any theoretical reason that will allay our doubt. Rather than searching for reasons we must instead contemplate the situation in which we find ourselves until we come directly to apprehend that the act in question is or is not our duty. As Prichard puts it:

'...suppose we come genuinely to doubt whether we ought, for example, to pay our debts, owing to a genuine doubt whether our previous conviction that we ought to do so is true, a doubt which can, in fact, only arise if we fail to remember the real nature of what we now call our past conviction. The only remedy lies in actually

[1] *Ibid.*, p. 28. Prichard is, thus, an intuitionist in the first as well as in the second sense of the term.

getting into a situation which occasions the obligation, or—if our imagination be strong enough—in imagining ourselves in that situation, and then letting our moral capacities of thinking do their work. Or, to put the matter generally, if we do doubt whether there is really an obligation to originate *A* in a situation *B*, the remedy lies not in any process of general thinking, but in getting face to face with a particular instance of the situation *B*, and then directly appreciating the obligation to originate *A* in that situation.'[1]

3. THE SELF-EVIDENCE OF OUR DUTIES

One comment should be made immediately about Prichard's view. This is that it avoids committing the deductive fallacy. Hume argued that moral theories, which purport to give arguments capable of justifying our beliefs about our duties, fall into the mistake of attempting to deduce an "ought" from an "is." Prichard caps Hume's point, and at the same time undercuts his criticism, by contending that the attempt to provide such arguments, besides being impossible, is unnecessary. To avoid Hume's skepticism, we have only to realize that our beliefs about our duty can be items of knowledge even though they are not supported by arguments.

Logically, Prichard does escape Hume. Before we conclude that he has solved the problem of moral knowledge, however, we must make sure that his view, in avoiding the deductive fallacy, does not run into insuperable difficulties elsewhere. As we have seen, Prichard contends that we can directly apprehend certain acts to be our duty. If such an apprehension is possible, then we should be able to say what these acts that we ought to do are. Assuming that Prichard has himself had experience in "directly appreciating" in various situations what he ought to do, we should expect him to be able to present some general conclusions about kinds of acts that he has found to be his duty. As a matter of fact he does do this in his article. Although he does not draw up any formal list of duties, he does make it clear in the course of his discussion that he knows the following kinds of acts to be our duty— to pay our debts, to tell the truth, to act justly, to refrain from hurting others without cause, to render a service in return for a service done us, to overcome our natural timidity, to overcome our natural greediness, to keep our promises, and to make ourselves better men.

Prichard believes it to be self-evident that these kinds of acts are

[1] *Ibid.*, pp. 36–37.

our duty. He has intuited them to be so and contends that, if we place ourselves, actually or imaginatively, in a situation like the one that he suggests in the quotation with which I concluded § 2, we shall do so also. Because we can know them to be our duty moral knowledge is shown to be possible. And if any of us should come to doubt that they really are our duty, all that we need (or can) do is to place ourselves in a situation in which one of them applies and we will, sooner or later, intuit that it is our duty.

I think that the best way to test Prichard's view is to try the experiment that he suggests. To do so I shall, with apologies, become autobiographical. Of the various kinds of intuitively apprehended duty taken from his article that I have just listed, all but two apply to everyone. The two exceptions, the duty to overcome our natural timidity and the duty to overcome our natural greediness, apply only to those of us who are by nature timid or greedy. I myself fall within this class. I mean, that is, that I am naturally timid. Thus it is easy for me to conduct the kind of imaginative experiment that Prichard recommends as the way to lead me to an appreciation of my duty to overcome my natural timidity. For I can recollect quite vividly past experiences in which I have been timid. I have deliberately relived these in memory, placing myself imaginatively in the same situation, and have waited for my moral capacities to do their work and reward me with a direct intuition of my duty to overcome my timidity. I have tried this experiment several times yet, I have to report, with no success.

What, then, has happened? Reporting as accurately as I can on these attempts I have made, here is what I found to occur. I had no difficulty in recognizing that my feeling of timidity often was groundless—that there was nothing in the situation to warrant the feeling. I found myself wanting to overcome my timidity and sometimes, by an act of will, deliberately suppressing it. But when I sought to find in the situation as I faced it a moral obligation to overcome my timidity, I found no intuition of duty forthcoming. Quite the contrary. The more I employed Prichard's method the more convinced I became that I should not succeed in gaining the intuition of a duty to overcome my timidity. I recognized a wish to be less timid, true, but this is quite different, as Prichard would be the first to agree, from recognizing a moral obligation to overcome my timidity.

What, if anything, does this autobiographical account prove? It certainly does not prove that I have no obligation to overcome my timidity. But it seems to me that it does cast serious doubt on Prichard's view about how we can come to know that certain things are our duty. Perhaps *he* can directly intuit a duty to overcome his natural timidity but *I* cannot—or, at least, have not. Yet he has said that all of us, by employing his method, can achieve the necessary intuition. Why was I not able to do so? Perhaps I have not tried long enough or hard enough. But, then, is the insight so hard to come by? Prichard implies just the contrary, indicating that it should present itself before my mind with the kind of immediacy and self-evidence that my apprehension that a three-sided figure must have three angles does.[1] And Ross writes of the "crystal-clear"[2] intuition of duty. But I find no intuition of duty, crystal-clear or otherwise. And the more I imaginatively contemplate the situation the more I doubt that I do have any such duty. Further consideration, rather than leading me toward the intuitive insight, leads me away from it. For me Prichard's method of recognizing our moral obligations, when applied to this case at least, results in failure. There is, of course, the possibility that I suffer from moral obtuseness.[3] Although I cannot rule out this possibility, I am willing to bet that, if it is the cause of my failure, then a lot of other people are as obtuse morally as I am.

But here a defender of Prichard might object, charging that the whole argument I have been giving is unfair. For I have chosen the weakest of the several different kinds of duty that Prichard mentions in his article, and attacked it. I admit that I have done this, and deliberately, too. Leaving aside the reason that this particular alleged duty is one that happens to fit my own situation as a person, it seems to me that a position like Prichard's asks for the kind of attack I have made. He contends that certain kinds of acts, by their very natures, are our duty. We can directly intuit that this is so and our apprehension is a case of knowledge. It is *self-evidently* true that they are our duty. These are formidable claims that Prichard is making, claims that should neither be lightly made nor lightly accepted. How does he substantiate them? As we have seen, when he comes to give examples of such duties, he includes the one I have challenged—mentioning it twice, in fact.[4] Unless we assume that his inclusion of this duty was a result of carelessness—an assumption that, considering Prichard's

---

[1] Cf. *ibid.*, p. 28.
[2] W. D. Ross, *Foundations of Ethics* (Oxford, 1939), p. 144.
[3] Cf. Prichard, "Does Moral Philosophy Rest on a Mistake?" *Op. cit.*, pp. 29–30, n. 1.
[4] The two references to this obligation appear on p. 29.

meticulousness as a thinker as well as the importance of the issue involved, seems hardly credible—we must conclude that he really believed that he did intuit it to be a duty. I can only record that I do not have the same intuition even though I have tried hard to do so. And if, as Prichard contends, the *only* appeal in such an issue is to intuition, then we have reached an impasse. But it is an impasse in which, as far as I am concerned, he has yet to make his case.

However, I do not want to rest my argument against the deontologists on criticisms of one weak point in their position. It is more important to decide whether their theory can stand at its strongest. In the attempt to determine this issue, I shall turn to the example that they believe to be, *par excellence*, a case of an intuitively apprehended, self-evident duty. This is the duty to keep promises.

4. THE DUTY TO KEEP PROMISES

In his book *Foundations of Ethics* Ross writes: "I would go so far as to say that the existence of an obligation arising from the making of a promise is so axiomatic that no moral universe can be imagined in which it would not exist."[1] Logically, Ross is not really going far in saying this because it is simply a consequence of his views on the obligation of promise-keeping. Both he and Prichard maintain that the reason why we ought to keep our promises lies in the very nature of a promise itself. The act of making a promise creates, of itself, a duty to fulfil the promise made. Therefore anyone anywhere, if he makes a promise, by that very act lays himself under an obligation to fulfil it. Is this true?[2]

Before we can answer this question I think we must be fairly clear about what a promise is. Here there is a danger. For in the paragraph preceding that from which the above quotation was taken Ross states that a promise is the "voluntary making of something obligatory on us which would not, or need not, have been obligatory before."[3] Now

---

[1] Ross, *op. cit.*, p. 77. The "obligation arising" is, naturally, that of fulfilling the promise.

[2] It should be noted that, for Ross, the obligation to fulfill a promise made is a *prima facie* duty rather than an actual duty (see above, p. 41). By this Ross means that, although the duty to keep our promises is *always* incumbent on us, this duty may be outweighed (but never obliterated) on occasion by some *more* incumbent duty. When no more pressing duty intervenes, then it is always our duty to keep a promise we have made. To evaluate the deontologists' position on the duty of promise-keeping, therefore, what we must try to determine is whether we always have a *prima facie* (rather than an actual) duty to keep our promises.

[3] *Ibid.*, p. 76. The "something obligatory" is the fulfilment of the promise.

if we take this statement to be a definition of "promise," as it seems in the context to be, there is no doubt that the making of a promise necessarily gives rise to an obligation. For the assertion that it does so is a tautology, to the effect that "the act of making something obligatory on us, when it is performed, gives rise to an obligation." However, the general tenor of Ross's argument in the subsequent discussion, as well as elsewhere in his writings, makes it quite evident that he does not mean to rest his case on an appeal to a tautology. Rather, he maintains that the relationship between the making of a promise and the duty of fulfilling it, although self-evidently necessary, is not analytic but synthetic. A proposition that asserts this relationship, thus, is "both synthetic and *a priori*."[1]

To avoid any possibility of lapsing into a tautology, perhaps it would be well to define a promise in such a way that no mention of any obligation of fulfilment appears in our definition. Let us say, then, that to make a promise is to pledge oneself to another to do some act in the future, or to give one's word to the other person that he will do the act. Or, as Ross puts it, a promise is "an intentional intimation to someone else that he can rely upon me to behave in a certain way..."[2] If anyone anywhere pledges himself or gives his word to another in this way, Ross maintains, it is self-evident that he has a *prima facie* duty to perform the act that he has pledged himself to do.

If one accepts the appeal to intuitive self-evidence as a basis for moral knowledge, I think he must admit that the deontologists can make a strong case in support of the view that we can know that we ought to keep our promises. For one of the most stubborn of moral convictions is the belief that the pledge we give when we make a promise is one that we have an obligation to fulfil. The recognition of this duty is not limited to a certain time or place but is one of the most universally accepted of all obligations. So the deontologists' thesis that the act of fulfilling a promise we have made is, by its very nature, one that we ought to do is a persuasive one. The question remains, however, Is it true? I should like to challenge its truth by appealing to the deontologists' own criterion of knowledge and arguing that it is not self-evident that we have a duty to keep a promise simply because "a promise is a promise."[3] If the act of fulfilling a promise we have made

---

[1] *Ibid.*, p. 320. Cf. W. D. Ross, *The Right and the Good* (Oxford, 1930), pp. 20–21, n. 1, 29–30, and 39–41.

[2] Ross, *Foundations of Ethics*, p. 77.

[3] Ross, *The Right and the Good*, p. 35.

is, by its nature, one that we ought to do, then no situation could arise in which, having made a promise, we should have no obligation to keep it. But are there not such situations? If there are, the deontologists' thesis that it is self-evident that a promise, by its very nature, ought to be kept is thrown into serious doubt.

Before I go any further I should make the point that is at issue here quite clear, because it is not at all what it might seem to be. My objection to the deontologists is *not* that there are actual situations in which a person who has made a promise may be morally justified in breaking that promise. For they do not deny this. Rather, they quite willingly grant that a person can justifiably break a promise he has made if doing so is necessary to the fulfilment of some other duty which, in the particular situation in question, is more incumbent on him than the obligation to fulfil his promise. (It is to accommodate this point that Ross makes his distinction between *prima facie* and actual duties—see p. 47 n. 2.) However, they would add, even in such a situation the obligation to keep the promise is not obliterated but only over-ridden. The person involved should, on moral grounds, regret having been forced to break it. So the case that I must make against the deontologists is quite an extreme one. To cast doubt on their thesis that we always have a *prima facie* (even though sometimes not an actual) duty to keep our promises simply because "a promise is a promise," I must try to show that there are situations in which a person who has made a promise has no duty *whatsoever* (not even a *prima facie* duty) to fulfil it. In such a situation he can break his promise with moral impunity.

With this important point made clear, I can state my objection to the deontologists' view by asking the following question: Are there ever situations in which one can be morally justified in making a "lying promise," a promise he does not intend to keep? I think there are good reasons for believing that such situations exist. Rather than multiplying examples, I shall limit myself to one situation, that of a promise made under a threat. The kind of case that comes immediately to mind here is the kidnapping situation. In many instances, as a perusal of newspaper "morgues" would bear out, kidnappers in their ransom instructions have stipulated that, if the parents are ever to see their child alive again, they must promise not to communicate with the police. The police, on the other hand, have made their opinion about kidnapping cases quite clear; if one should ever have his child kidnapped, he should communicate with the police immediately, regardless of any promises made to the kidnapper. In fact, the police probably would recommend a "lying promise," for its value in giving the kidnapper a false sense of security. Cases like this have occurred. In some the victims have kept the promises they have made; in others they have broken them. How are we to judge them morally? Do we think that the police, if they advise a "lying promise," are encouraging an immoral act? Do we believe that the victims have *any* moral obligation to fulfill the promise they have made to the kidnapper? What are our actual moral convictions about such cases? If we were to put these questions to the "plain man" (to whom Ross generally appeals in support of his moral intuitions),[1] I doubt that we should get a completely unambiguous reply. However, I am quite sure that the general opinion would go against Ross. I am sure enough of this, in fact, to predict that, if the citizens of our (or his) country were polled on the questions I have just asked, they would vote overwhelmingly against him.

But someone might ask, What would that prove? The fact that no one recognizes an obligation in this situation does not prove it non-existent, for everyone might be mistaken. Granted; they might be. Because that is possible I would not be willing to draw any absolute conclusions about our duty in this (or any other) situation from a consensus of the moral beliefs of the citizenry. But where does this leave Ross? He has maintained that it is self-evident that promises ought to be kept. In support of his view he appeals to the moral convictions of the plain man, assuming that what the plain man accepts in such matters must be true. "The main moral convictions of the plain man seem to me to be, not opinions which it is for philosophy to prove or disprove, but knowledge from the start..."[2] But, if I am correct about the outcome of the poll I have suggested, the plain man almost surely would let Ross down here. If one believes the main moral convictions of the plain man really to be knowledge, then he cannot maintain, as Ross does, that the act of fulfilling a promise we have made is, by its very nature, one that we ought to do.

But Ross, even though he might admit my judgment about the moral views of the plain man in this situation, might still object to my conclusion, arguing that my illustration is unfair because a promise made under a threat is not a *real* promise. Certainly the situation I have envisaged is an unusual one, but is it unusual enough to sustain this

[1] Cf. *ibid.*, pp. 17, *passim.*
[2] *Ibid.*, pp. 20–21, n. 1.

objection? Or is the objection itself really relevant? The answer to these questions turns on what a *real* promise is. If we accept the definition of a promise that I gave at the beginning of the discussion—and Ross's second definition, which I quoted, is almost identical with mine—[1] I do not see how we can deny that a promise made under a threat is a real promise. For it clearly satisfies both our definitions. If we do deny that it is a real promise, we must do so on the grounds that the definitions are not complete. What, then, is lacking in them? To support the objection I have just raised on Ross's behalf, the answer would have to be: They make no mention of the circumstances in which a promise must be made in order to qualify as a real promise. Because a promise made in circumstances in which the promiser is under a threat does not qualify as a real promise, we have no obligation to fulfil it.

But can the deontologists hold both that the duty to keep our promises rests on the intrinsic nature of a promise and that an act that satisfies the definition which they themselves give of a promise, because it is made under a threat, is not really a promise? Let us for argument's sake grant that they can and see what follows. Suppose a person asks a friend to lend him some money. The friend, knowing from bitter past experience the shortness of the would-be borrower's memory once a loan is made, agrees to lend the money but only on condition that the borrower will sign a promissory note, mortgaging his possessions, for the amount loaned. If the borrower signs the note, he will be making a promise under a threat, promising to return the money loaned, and threatened that, if he fails to keep his promise, he will be stripped of his possessions. Does he have any moral obligation to fulfil his promise? The deontologists, I am sure, would answer in the affirmative. And in this answer the plain man would certainly agree with them. But, if this is correct, then the fact that it is made under a threat does not prevent an act that satisfies their definition of a promise from being a real promise. So the question remains: What reason could the deontologists give for holding that in the case of the kidnapped child no real promise was made? I believe they could be forced finally to the admission that it cannot be a real promise because we do not have any duty at all (not even a *prima facie* duty) to fulfil it. But, if they take this line, they must give up any pretence that our "intuition" of a duty to keep our promises can yield an item of moral knowledge. For the proposition "We always have a duty to keep our promises" now must mean "We

[1] See above, p. 48.

always have a duty to do those acts—which we call keeping our promises—that we have a duty to do." And this is a tautology. Or, to put the point in another way, to be an item of knowledge the proposition "We always have a (*prima facie*) duty to keep our promises" must, as Ross says, be both synthetic and *a priori*. My case of the kidnapped child shows that it is not *a priori*; the objection to my case that I have raised can make it *a priori* only at the expense of admitting that it is not synthetic.

Prichard and Ross might object to my conclusion in quite another way, arguing that the judgment of the plain man in this case, assuming that I have gauged it correctly, is in error. For the duty to fulfil a promise always remains, even though that promise has been made under a threat. If they did adopt this position, how could they defend it? I think that what they would have to say, finally, is something like this: Regardless of what other people conclude, we see that the duty remains. They would have, in other words, to base their decision on their own personal intuitive insight.

The appeal to personal intuition as a basis for denying the general consensus of society in this case can, I think, be criticized on two counts. In the first place it runs counter to one of the main assumptions of the deontologists, that people will agree in their basic moral insights. Both Prichard and Ross compare our apprehension of moral truths with our apprehension of mathematical truths, Ross writing, for example, that "both in mathematics and in ethics we have certain crystal-clear intuitions from which we build up all that we can know about the nature of numbers and the nature of duty."[1] It would be inconceivable that anyone who takes this statement seriously could then go on to assert that his personal moral intuitions can be correct even when they contradict those of society as a whole. To do so would be to charge the majority of mankind with an obtuseness of monumental proportions, comparable in magnitude to a general insistence—to use the mathematical analogy—that two plus two equals five.

Furthermore, even if the deontiologsts could, consistently with their general view, ever justify a radical departure from the moral pronouncements of the group, would such a departure take place in the situation being considered? What verdict does personal insight yield in this case? To answer this question I must again become autobiographical. Employing Prichard's method, I must put myself (imagina-

---

[1] Ross, *Foundations of Ethics*, p. 144. Cf. Prichard, "Does Moral Philosophy Rest on a Mistake?" *Op. cit.*, p. 28.

tively) in the place of a parent whose child has been abducted and who has given a promise to the kidnappers not to communicate with the police. If I try now to appreciate an obligation to keep that promise, I find that I fail. I recognize reasons for not communicating with the police, mainly a fear that such action will lead to the death of my child, but, try as I may, I find myself unable to recognize any obligation to the kidnappers. My failure may be a result simply of a lack of imagination or moral insight but, when the reality of our duties must be judged by Prichard's method, all that I can do is to report the results I obtain when I employ that method, adding that I am quite sure that most people would get the same results I have.

To some my case may still remain suspect, because it is based on an appeal to a single and admittedly unusual situation. I think the first shortcoming (that I have given only a single example) can be overcome fairly easily. For instance, do soldiers captured in war always have a *prima facie* obligation to keep a promise made to their captors not to attempt to escape? Or do I have any *prima facie* obligation to give my friend a gun I have promised him if I learn he is planning to shoot himself with it? (My point in these questions, it should be remembered, must be not simply to imply that, whatever our obligation to keep our promise in such situations may be, it is clearly over-ridden by other considerations, but rather to imply that in these situations we may have no obligation to keep the promise at all.) As for the second point (that my example is unusual), I would readily agree with the deontologists that ordinarily we do have a duty to keep our promises therefore any situation in which this obligation does not hold is bound to be an unusual one. But this very agreement implies the point I am trying to make against them. The reason why the obligation disappears in these cases is that the situation *is* unusual. In other words, the circumstances in which the promise is made, or is to be kept, determine whether or not it ought to be kept. But the deontologists cannot grant this because, for them, the obligation to keep a promise rests not on circumstances at all but on the very nature of a promise. If my objections hold, Ross's statement with which I began this section, "I would go so far as to say that the existence of an obligation arising from the making of a promise is so axiomatic that no moral universe can be imagined in which it would not exist," is false. Thus the very case on which the deontologists believe their thesis of the intuitive self-evidence of our duties to find its firmest grounding has proved to be vulnerable. If they cannot justify the belief that promises, by their very nature, ought to be kept, then there seems small chance that they will have any more success with our other beliefs about what we ought to do.

5. INTUITION AND GENERALIZATION

If we agree, against Ross, that it is not true that we ought to keep our promises simply because "a promise is a promise," can we conclude without further ado that it is impossible to substantiate our beliefs about our duties by an appeal to direct intuition? Prichard, I think, might object to such a conclusion on the grounds that our case against Ross does not eliminate the possibility of intuitive moral knowledge. For such knowledge, rather than being an apprehension of general truths ("Promises as such ought to be kept"), is an apprehension of particular truths ("I ought to keep *this* promise I have made"). Whether Prichard would actually defend such a position I am not sure; it seems, however, to be compatible with the method he advocates as the way to apprehend a moral obligation. As I indicated earlier in the discussion (§ 2), he believes that the only way to "appreciate" an obligation is to place ourselves (either actually or imaginatively) in a situation which "occasions" the obligation and then let our "moral capacities" do their work, giving us the proper intuitive awareness of the obligation. Now the results of such a procedure are bound to be, not an appreciation of the general dutifulness of a certain kind of action (keeping our promises) but an appreciation of our duty to keep *this* particular promise we have made. Because we can intuit an obligation to keep a particular promise (or do some other particular act in a given situation) we are justified in concluding that we can know not only that we have duties but also what our actual duty in a given situation is, even though we are unable to generalize this knowledge in the way that Ross attempts to do. Thus moral knowledge in the particular, at least, is vindicated.

To judge this hypothetical argument of Prichard's, we must decide whether what he would call the intuitive apprehension of a particular duty can support the claim to yield an item of moral knowledge. I do not think it can, for the following reason: Let us suppose a situation in which a person, having made a promise, comes to doubt whether he really ought to keep it. To decide the issue, he employs Prichard's method of direct intuition. But he gets conflicting results. At one time he clearly intuits a duty to keep the promise. At another he just as clearly intuits that it is his duty not to keep it. Prichard certainly could not object to this example because he would have to admit (1) that we do not always (*i.e.*, in every particular situation) have a duty to keep our promises, (2) that we are just as capable of intuiting in a given situation that we have a duty not to do a particular act as we are of intuiting that we have a duty to do it, and (3) that the kind of situation I have hypothesized is commonly experienced by conscientious people, who, in their attempts to determine what their duty is, often find themselves, especially in complex situations in which different and opposing moral claims press for their attention, first clearly apprehending their duty to be one thing and then, after further reflection, as clearly apprehending it to be something else.

What conclusions can we derive from my example? When the person in doubt, following Prichard's method, intuits a duty to keep the promise he has made, then, Prichard maintains, he *knows* that he ought to do so, his intuition justifying his knowledge claim. On the other hand, when he directly intuits that he ought not to keep the promise, he *knows* that he ought not to do so. Since knowledge can only be of the truth, it follows that Prichard must hold it to be true in such a situation both that the person ought and that he ought not to keep the promise. But these assertions contradict each other.

To answer this argument Prichard would have to show that people never have contradictory "intuitions" of what they ought to do in any given situation. But this he cannot show. For the evidence against him is overwhelming.

To summarize briefly the somewhat long argument of the last three sections, what I have been trying to do is to cast doubt on the deontologists' thesis that we can know, because we directly intuit, either that we ought to do certain acts or certain types of act. Although I have raised logical objections to their views, my main criticism has rested on an appeal to intuition rather than logic. For this reason I cannot call it conclusive. It is possible that Prichard and Ross do know that they have a duty to overcome their natural timidity and always to keep their promises because they immediately apprehend such a duty and that my failure to have the same intuitions is a result simply of a deficiency in my moral insight. But the question remains: Can we take their claims to intuitive certainty seriously enough to base a theory of moral knowledge on them? I doubt very much that the deontologists' testimony would have much weight with the moral skeptic, or even with a non-committed, but critically-minded inquirer trying to find a justification for our moral beliefs. For even while admitting that my objections to the deontologists, which rest on an appeal to intuition, are not conclusive, I would add that their own affirmations, because they rest on the same appeal, equally fall short of conclusiveness. If this is true, we could agree that people do have what they call moral intuitions and still raise the question: Do these "intuitions" really yield items of knowledge? Rather than pursuing this question further here, I shall postpone it until Chapter VI, in which I shall return to intuitionism as a theory of moral knowledge.

Although the deontologists' position does not, in my opinion, provide an acceptable alternative to moral skepticism, it does accomplish one lesser, but still important thing. It succeeds in escaping the deductive fallacy. By holding that our duties are self-evident, it avoids the logical fallacy of attempting to deduce an "ought" from an "is" by trying to give reasons to justify these duties.

6. RIGHTNESS AND DUTY

The view that I have just been examining, that certain acts, because of their very nature, are *right* or our *duty* (or *morally obligatory* or the acts we *ought* to do) and can be apprehended to be so by direct moral intuition, is the only theory of moral obligation that the deontologists explicitly hold. Nevertheless, I believe that another, slightly different theory can be derived by extrapolation from their position. The need for such an alternative view becomes apparent as soon as we recognize an important, but easily overlooked distinction in the meanings of the main moral concepts that we have been discussing in this chapter. Because they did not recognize the distinction in question until after they had developed their theory, the deontologists have not followed out its implications for the problem of moral knowledge. I shall do this briefly, in the remainder of the chapter.

The concepts in question are those I have italicized at the beginning of the last paragraph, "right" and "duty" (with its various synonyms). What does it mean to say of an act that it is right? Does it mean the same as to say that the act is our duty or morally obligatory or the act that we ought to do? Or do the things mean something different? In *The Right and the Good* Ross writes "...if we turn to the sort of moral judgment in which we do use the word 'right,' such as 'this is the right act,' it is clear that by this we mean 'this act is the act *that ought to be done,*' 'this act is *morally obligatory.*'"[1] I think that Ross is mistaken here. For the concepts in question do not mean the same thing. When we say "This is the right act," we are using the term "right" to characterize the act. Rightness is an attribute which we believe that the act itself possesses. As Ross puts it, "The rightness of an act... is intrinsic to the act, depending solely on its nature."[2] Turning to the other concepts, it seems from Ross's statement that they, too, are attributes of the act in question. It is the act that "ought to be done," or that is "morally obligatory." But are these, like "right," really, as they appear grammatically to be, attributes of the act? Prichard, like Ross, seems to think that they are. For he writes: "The word 'ought' refers to actions and to actions alone."[3] My reason for believing that Prichard and Ross are mistaken in identifying these concepts, making them all attributes of acts, can be explained most easily by returning to the quotation from Ross. When he says that one equivalent of "This is the right act" is "This act is the act that ought to be done," the grammatical form of the second statement suggests that a characteristic, which might be called its "ought-to-be-doneness," is being predicated of the act. But I think Ross would agree that such a suggestion is misleading, being a consequence mainly of his use of the passive voice. Put in a form more expressive of what he really means the statement would read "This act is the act that I ought to do" or, even less ambiguously, "I ought to do this act." As these restatements make increasingly clear, the "ought," rather than referring to the act, refers to *me*, the agent. This point becomes even more apparent when we look at Ross's other equivalent to "This is the right act," namely, "This act is morally obligatory." Obviously the act does not, and cannot, possess any such characteristic as "moral obligatoriness." For such a conceptual monstrosity could have no existence outside of the theories of philosophers. What we must mean when we say "This act is morally obligatory," if we mean anything, is "I have a moral obligation to do this act."[4]

---

[1] Ross, *The Right and the Good,* p. 3. Ross goes on to point out a minor difference in the meaning (or in the application) of the two concepts but concludes that, because the difference is unimportant, he will disregard it (pp. 3-4).

[2] *Ibid.,* p. 132.

[3] Prichard, "Does Moral Philosophy Rest on a Mistake?" *Op. cit.,* p. 24.

[4] Both Prichard and Ross have (in later writings) recognized the distinction I am making here. Prichard, for example, writes: "We are apt to think of an obligation to do some action as if it were, like its goodness or badness, a sort of quality or character of the action. Just as we think that when we say of some action which we could do that it would be good, or, again, bad, we are stating that, in a wide sense of the term 'character,' it would have a certain character, so we are apt to think that when we say of it that we are bound, or bound not, to do it, we are stating that it would have a certain

Therefore, instead of saying that "This is the right act" and "This act is the act that ought to be done" *mean* the same thing, the most that Ross can say is that the second statement follows from the first. From a characteristic of the act, its rightness, something which is not a characteristic of the act, my duty to perform it, follows. Or, in other words, I ought to do the act *because* it is right. But this leaves us with the question: How can we justify the "because"? Why is the fact that the act is right a good reason for the conclusion that I have a duty to do it?

7. FROM RIGHTNESS TO DUTY

The problem facing us here should by now be apparent. Having distinguished between the meaning of rightness and duty, we are asking what kind of an argument we can use to derive our duty to do an act from the knowledge that the act is right. Any such argument must be deductive in form and it must contain an "ought" in its conclusion. But if its premises contain only statements about right acts—and rightness does not, we have decided, mean the same as "oughtness"—then our argument will be a *non sequitur*. To validate the argument we would have to insert an "ought" into the premises, but this "ought" in its turn would have to be justified by a further argument, and we would be led into an infinite regress. We have, in other words, run afoul of the deductive fallacy. It is equally as impossible to deduce our duties from the rightness of acts as it is to do so from the goodness of the consequences of those acts.

There is one way in which we could derive our duties from the rightness of acts and still escape committing the deductive fallacy. This is by an appeal to intuitive self-evidence. We could maintain that it is not necessary to employ any argument at all to establish our conclusion because we directly apprehend that we have a duty to do right acts.

Since I have already examined the deontologists' appeal to intuition at length in this chapter, and shall return to the subject again in Chapter VI, I shall not discuss it further here. However, I would like

character, for which the proper term would be 'ought-to-be-doneness' or 'ought-not-to-be-doneness.' And this tendency is fostered by our habit of using the terms 'right' and 'wrong' as equivalents for 'ought' and 'ought not.' ... But, as we recognize when we reflect, there are no such characteristics of an action as ought-to-be-doneness and ought-not-to-be-doneness." "Duty and Ignorance of Fact," *Proceedings of the British Academy*, XVIII (1932), 90. Cf. Ross, *Foundations of Ethics*, p. 56.

to make one point. In the theory that I considered first (§'s 2–4), the deontologists maintain that it is self-evidently true that certain acts, like promise-keeping, are our duties. We can intuitively apprehend a connection between the nature of the act itself and our duty to do it. In the theory now being considered, to establish the reality of duty, we must intuit, not one, but two connections—(1) between the nature of the act (*e.g.*, being an act of promise-keeping) and the act's rightness, the act being right because it is of this nature, and then (2) between its rightness and our duty to perform it. Anyone who is reluctant to accept the appeal made to intuition in the first theory, thus, has twice the reason for rejecting the second.

In this and the preceding chapter I have examined, in their contemporary formulations, the two major traditional ways of justifying our beliefs about what we ought to do. Neither, I think it fair to say, is successful in answering the arguments of the moral skeptics. The alternative replies they offer consist either in presenting an argument in defense of their conclusions about our duties, in which case they commit the deductive fallacy, or else in falling back on an appeal to a direct intuition of duty, in which case they leave unanswered the question, How can we be sure that the content of what we believe we intuit is knowledge? The argument so far, thus, raises serious doubts as to the possibility of finding, within the limits of traditional moral philosophy, any acceptable alternative to moral skepticism. Perhaps the answer then must be to abandon traditional philosophy. This, at least, is the opinion of an important and influential group of contemporary philosophers, to whose views on the problem of moral knowledge I shall now turn.

CHAPTER IV

A NEW POINT OF VIEW

The conclusions we reached in the last two chapters seem to leave small hope that any solution to the problem of moral knowledge can be found within traditional moral theory. Perhaps the time has come to abandon traditional philosophy altogether and approach our problem from a radically new point of view. Such, indeed, would be the advice of a very important contemporary group of philosophers, mainly at Oxford. This group, whom A. G. N. Flew refers to as "the avant-garde of Oxford philosophy since the war,"[1] is responsible for the most exciting and influential development, with the possible exception of existentialism, in Western philosophy in the past twenty years. In this chapter I shall describe the way in which these philosophers have approached the problem of moral knowledge and the answers they have given to it.

1. OXFORD PHILOSOPHY

The movement I am about to describe has no official name. It has been referred to variously as "Oxford philosophy," "Oxford analysis," "linguistic analysis," "ordinary language philosophy," and so on. For purposes of my discussion, I shall use the term "analysis" to refer to the movement and "analysts" to its members. (I should make it clear that I am using this term simply as a tag for purposes of convenience and do not mean to imply that anyone who considers himself an analytic philosopher must accept the views of the Oxford group.)

But the absence of any name for the movement has a positive significance. For many analysts refuse to consider themselves part of a special group or movement at all. They resent being tagged, not only because they wish to set themselves apart from traditional philosophy with its "schools," forever engaged in fruitless internecine warfare, but also because they have, as individuals, often reached conclusions quite

---

[1] A. G. N. Flew, "Philosophy and Language," *The Philosophical Quarterly*, 5 (1955), 23.

different from those of other analysts on substantive philosophical issues (including the problem of moral knowledge). Although it is true that there are important differences of opinion among analysts and although one may sympathize with their desire to dissociate themselves from the traditional "schools" approach to philosophy, nevertheless I think that, if we are to appreciate the significance of analysis, we must view it as a philosophical movement. For the analysts have one thing in common, which is far more important than the differences between them. This is a particular, and novel, approach to philosophy itself, a new way of "doing" philosophy. And it is the analysts' way of doing philosophy, rather than the specific conclusions that any given analyst reaches by means of this method, that makes analysis the important movement that it is.

Because analysis is a contemporary philosophical movement, it is in a state of constant change and development. This makes it somewhat difficult for the reviewer who attempts to describe it. No characterization can be completely adequate and any attempt to state unequivocally *the* complete analyst position can be challenged by quotations drawn from the writings of philosophers who are clearly members of the group. The best one can do is to concentrate on the central features of the position, particularly those theses which most sharply distinguish analysis from traditional philosophy. In the field of moral philosophy the task is made relatively easy by the existence of several books written by analyst authors which, though differing in various details, are in agreement on the basic assumptions of analysis, as these apply to moral philosophy. I shall use two of these books as the main basis for the discussion that follows. Before I turn to moral philosophy, however, I must first give a brief review of analysis as a whole, for the views expressed by the analytic moral philosophers are the application to a special field of a general philosophical point of view so can be understood only within the context of that point of view. My review of analysis here will include only its salient and distinguishing features and these will be presented in summary form, without qualifications or comment, simply as a background for my detailed discussion of analytic moral philosophy in Chapter V.

2. THE REVOLUTION IN PHILOSOPHY

The analysts consider themselves to be revolutionary. In fact the development of analysis has been referred to as a "revolution in philosophy" and for at least some analysts the term "traditional philosophy" has become a pejorative. In their belief that analysis is revolutionary I think the analysts are quite right. I emphasize this point because there has been a tendency in the last few years, even among some of the analysts themselves, to play down the novelty of their view, to the point sometimes of suggesting that many traditional philosophers, unknown to themselves, really were proto-analysts. But to minimize its revolutionary character is to deny the very thing that makes analysis philosophically exciting and significant, leaving it in danger of becoming just a dreary and pointless pursuit of trivial asnwers to generally trivial questions.

Analysis is revolutionary not because it is a novel philosophical theory but rather because it is a new conception of the nature of philosophy itself, a radically different idea of what philosophy is and what philosophers should do. According to the analysts, traditional philosophers have generally conceived it to be the task of philosophy to explain the world. In fulfilment of this task philosophers formulated theories which they believed to be true accounts of the nature of Reality. And they criticized the theories formulated by other philosophers, arguing that these theories were false. All of this, the analysts contend, is a mistake. For the search for Truth is a philosophical dead end. Philosophers must abandon it, giving up with it all attempts to develop explanatory theories. (The job of advancing such theories, most analysts believe, is the province of empirical science.)[1] In place of formulating theories, philosophers should devote their energy to simple description. And what is it that they are to describe? The actual workings of ordinary language, the analysts reply. In the words of Ludwig Wittgenstein: "We must do away with all *explanation*, and description alone must take its place. And this description gets its power of illumination—i.e. its purpose—from the philosophical problems. These are, of course, not empirical problems; they are solved, rather, by looking into the workings of our language...."[2]

The kernel of the analytic revolution in philosophy is contained in this quotation taken from Wittgenstein. To appreciate the analysts' point of view one must understand whatever they say in terms of it. Although the quotation provides the key to analysis, it is not, however,

---

[1] Cf. G. J. Warnock, "Analysis and Imagination," in *The Revolution in Philosophy* (London, 1957), pp. 122–123.

[2] L. Wittgenstein, *Philosophical Investigations*, trans. G. E. M. Anscombe (Oxford, 1953), § 109.

the whole of it. The best introduction to the rest of analysis is through the writings of Wittgenstein, for Wittgenstein is the source of most of the views regarding philosophy which form the basis of the analytic position. Before turning to Wittgenstein himself, I should insert a remark about the relationship between analysis and another recent, and revolutionary philosophical movement—logical positivism. Many philosophers on the outside, and particularly those who are critical of analysis, often confuse or identify it with logical positivism. This is an error. Although the movements are related to each other—Wittgenstein was associated with the Vienna Circle for a time and his early book, the *Tractatus Logico-Philosophicus*, is positivistic in its general tenor—it is essential to distinguish carefully between the views of the "later" Wittgenstein, which receive their fullest expression in his *Philosophical Investigations* and which form the basis for analysis, and positivism. For the later Wittgenstein and his analytic followers the verification principle of the positivists is just another philosophical theory. In their adherence to it the positivists mark themselves as traditional philosophers, making the same basic mistake as the rest. Revolutionary though it may have seemed to many traditionalists, positivism, in the eyes of the analysts, is simply a recent, although quite violent, example of the internecine warfare of traditional philosophy, which their own later, and more complete, revolution has rendered otiose. That the analysts dissociate themselves from the positivists while admitting a joint debt with them to Wittgenstein is made clear in the following summary statement by the Oxford philosopher, A. Quinton, who writes:

"We must clearly distinguish between two kinds of analytic philosophy, both of which owe a very great deal to Wittgenstein, and both of which are, in quite different ways, 'linguistic.'

In the first place there is the formalist view of Carnap, and the Vienna Circle. They saw their task as the purification and reconstruction of language on the model of the *Principia Mathematica* of Russell and Whitehead. *This* is the specially 'anti-metaphysical' kind of analytic philosophy, and the proper bearer of the name 'logical positivism.'

In the second place there is current Oxford philosophy—the philosophy of 'ordinary language'–which is literal, rather than formal in its bias; which seeks to remove philosophical perplexity by the achievement of a fuller understanding of the language we actually use."[1]

[1] A. Quinton, "Philosophy and Beliefs," *The Twentieth Century*, 157 (1955), 512.

3. WITTGENSTEIN

P. F. Strawson, writing a review of Wittgenstein's *Philosophical Investigations*, concludes with the following evaluation:

"Right or wrong, Wittgenstein's particular doctrines are of the greatest interest and importance. But the value of the book as a model of philosophical method is greater still. (Here I do *not* refer to idiosyncracies of style and form.) It will consolidate the philosophical revolution for which, more than anyone else, its author was responsible."[1]

In this section I shall give a brief sketch of the philosophical method originated by Wittgenstein which, as Strawson rightly concludes, is his most important contribution to philosophy and the basis on which the philosophical revolution that he inaugurated rests. Since my interest here is in the moral philosophy of the analysts, I shall limit my account of Wittgenstein to an exposition of those features of his thought which are essential to an understanding of the later developments in moral philosophy based on it.

According to Wittgenstein traditional philosophers as a group are guilty of the error of attempting to theorize or to explain the world. In their pursuit of theoretical explanations, philosophers have been led inevitably into absurdity, accepting conclusions that in their non-philosophical moments they simply would not take seriously. (A classical confirmation of Wittgenstein's point is given by Hume in the conclusion of Book I of the *Treatise*, in which he poignantly describes his own turmoil of soul when he contrasts the conclusions he has reached in his study with the view of the world he accepts as an ordinary human being.) But what leads philosophers to their strange and unbelievable conclusions? The source of their errors lies in language itself; they are, as Wittgenstein puts it, "bewitched" by language. Instead of simply accepting our language, they search for hidden meanings behind what we say. They ask themselves, What is the *real*

---

[1] P. F. Strawson, "Philosophical Investigations," *Mind*, N.S.—63 (1954), 99. Some people—including, probably, Wittgenstein himself—would take issue with the view expressed by Strawson here (and by Quinton in the preceding quotation) on the grounds that the Oxford analysts are not the heirs of the Wittgensteinian philosophical revolution but its perverters. Not only would it be beyond the scope of my book to discuss this complicated issue, but I think that I am justified in following the line I have taken for at least two reasons: (1) It is an historical fact that Oxford analysis has developed primarily out of the thought of Wittgenstein and (2) the analysts themselves, whether rightly or wrongly, do consider their views to be a true expression and expansion of those of Wittgenstein.

meaning of some word or expression we use? In pursuit of this essence of meaning, they pull the word out of its context of use and examine it in isolation. The philosopher's urge to explain aggravates this error. In his search for a theoretical explanation he tries to find a single formula in terms of which all of our language uses can be expressed. He assumes that it is possible (as Wittgenstein himself did in his *Tractatus-Logico-Philosophicus*) to construct an ideal language which can express everything we have to say. When he finds that our language cannot be forced into such a strait-jacket he banishes all the recalcitrant expressions as meaningless.

The philosopher is not, however, alone to blame for his extravagances. Language itself must share the responsibility for them, for it often tricks the philosopher into committing his absurdities. The root trouble lies in the grammatical form of our language, which is insufficient for the needs of actual use. To take a simple example, the words "believe" and "walk" are both verbs. Verbs, grammatically classified, are action words. So grammar leads us to assume that these two words should be analyzed in the same way, with the strange result that we conclude that believing is a kind of activity like walking. Wittgenstein contends that many philosophical absurdities can be traced back to just such simple errors as this. Hence he is led to conclude: "When we [traditional philosophers] do philosophy, we are like savages, primitive people, who hear the expressions of civilized men, put a false interpretation on them, and then draw the queerest conclusions from it."[1]

Although he believed that the conclusions reached by traditional philosophers are usually nonsensical, Wittgenstein was not content, as the positivists were, with a cavalier dismissal of them. For these conclusions, and particularly the errors which have led to them, are not trivial. In their endless pursuit of will-o-the-wisps, philosophers are not simply being perverse. Rather, they have been tricked into their pursuit by the nature of the language we use. And their errors are important because our language is important.

"The problems arising through a misinterpretation of our forms of language have the character of *depth*. They are deep disquietudes; their roots are as deep in us as the forms of our language and their significance is as great as the importance of our language.—Let us ask ourselves: why do we feel a grammatical joke to be *deep*? (And that is what the depth of philosophy is.)"[2]

[1] L. Wittgenstein, *op. cit.*, § 194.
[2] *Ibid.*, § 111.

Although it leads them into absurdity, philosophers seem unable to resist the temptation to philosophize. The urge to formulate theories of explanation becomes compulsive with them (a fact of which Hume's testimony bears eloquent witness). Here Wittgenstein reaches a novel and to some, perhaps, a shocking conclusion—that the activity of philosophizing (in the traditional sense) is pathological, a sickness of which the victim needs to be cured. One interpreter of his thought, G. J. Warnock, suggests that Wittgenstein believed traditional philosophers to be insane.[1] In a sense, I suppose, Warnock is right. However, I do not think that Warnock means (or should mean) to imply by this that Wittgenstein considered traditional philosophers to be mad, in the strict sense. For I seriously doubt that he would have recommended institutionalization for the great thinkers of the past. If, in interpreting Wittgenstein, we speak of philosophy as insanity, we should perhaps emphasize that by insanity we mean such things as "the bewitchment of our intelligence by means of language,"[2] "deep disquietudes," and the compulsive urge to theorize.

How do we cure ourselves of this sickness that is philosophy? By giving up our attempts to theorize and devoting our energies, instead, to the description of the ways in which language is actually used, Wittgenstein replies. "Philosophy may in no way interfere with the actual use of language; it can in the end only describe it."[3] If we free ourselves of the urge to theorize, cast off our preconceptions about language, and turn to gaze with unbiassed eye at our language as it actually functions in our everyday life, we will see it in an entirely new perspective. The main conclusions about language that Wittgenstein derived from his own observations were the following: Language is a natural activity in which human beings engage, as natural as walking or eating. Like these activities it functions to satisfy various human needs and fulfil various human purposes. Our language is like a tool box filled with tools; some tools work well for certain jobs, others for others. But we run into trouble if we try to use the wrong tool for the job we have to do or if (as traditional philosophers have usually done) we demand that all tools do the same job. In another metaphor, Wittgenstein calls the various uses to which we put our words "language-games."[4] As in ordinary games, there are rules governing the

---

[1] Cf. G. J. Warnock, *English Philosophy Since 1900* (London, 1958), p. 88.
[2] L. Wittgenstein, *op. cit.*, § 109.
[3] *Ibid.*, § 124.
[4] *Ibid.*, § 23.

way in which our words are to be used in each game and these rules
are determined by the purpose of that game. Wittgenstein says that
there are countless such language-games, or countless uses to which
language is actually put. In *Philosophical Investigations* he gives a long
list of these, including giving orders, describing an object, making up
a story, telling a joke, cursing, praying, and many others.[1] Although
we use language in different ways in our various language-games,
these uses are not totally unlike each other; rather there are, as
Wittgenstein puts it, certain "family resemblances"[2] among them. To
give an unlikely illustration, there is probably some similarity in our
purposes when we use certain words either to curse or to pray.

Such, very briefly, is Wittgenstein's revolutionary alternative to
traditional philosophy. From his new point of view Wittgenstein believes that he can expose the errors that have vitiated past philosophy.
But this is not his main purpose. Nor is it to find solutions for old
philosophical problems. Rather his purpose is to make it clear that no
solutions are required. Philosophical problems are not to be solved but
dissolved. Where traditional philosophers sought for explanations,
Wittgenstein contends that there is nothing that needs explaining.
"Philosophy simply puts everything before us, and neither explains
nor deduces anything.—Since everything lies open to view, there is
nothing to explain."[3] Because this is true, philosophy, in the traditional
sense, is unnecessary. Like capitalism, it is to be buried and Wittgenstein is its grave digger.[4]

But how are traditional philosophers to be convinced of this?
Wittgenstein does not claim that he can argue them out of their
superstitions. To accept his point of view they must simply "see the
light." Or, to use Warnock's apt analogy, abandoning traditional
philosophy and accepting Wittgenstein is "comparable rather with
conversion than with the detection of error."[5]

---

[1] Cf. *ibid.*

[2] *Ibid.*, § 67.

[3] *Ibid.*, § 126.

[4] Several of Wittgenstein's followers have gone beyond him at this point. Although
they accept his view that an important function of the new philosophy is to cure us of
our disease of traditional philosophy, they believe that there are other things than this
that philosophers can do. For example, several have become interested in the description of our various uses of language, not just for its therapeutic value, but as an
end in itself. In the hands of these analysts, particularly J. L. Austin, the examination
of the ways in which we use certain words has been pursued with great rigor and
thoroughness and the ability to distinguish the slightest nuances of usage has been
developed into a fine art.

[5] G. J. Warnock, *op. cit.*, p. 78.

4. ANALYSIS AND MORAL PHILOSOPHY

Wittgenstein wrote very little on the subject of moral philosophy. Quite the opposite is true of his followers. Among the analysts moral philosophy has been a subject of great interest, discussed in innumerable journal articles since the war and in several books, particularly in the last dozen years. The analytic moral philosophers have taken the general philosophical views of Wittgenstein and have attempted to apply them to the special field of morality, using the new method to gain a fresh approach to the entire subject and hence to avoid many of the problems that have beset traditional moral philosophy. Like Wittgenstein, the analytic moral philosophers appreciate fully the revolutionary character of their new method and have emphasized the contrast between themselves and the traditional writers. A notable expression of this contrast, and of the Wittgensteinian view that traditional philosophy is a superstition from which we must be converted, appears in S. E. Toulmin's *An Examination of The Place of Reason in Ethics*, the first major, book-length application of Wittgenstein's views to moral philosophy. After a beginning section of his book devoted to a criticism of "the traditional approaches" to the problem of moral knowledge—in which he concludes that the objectivists, subjectivists, and imperativists, despite the differences between them, all commit the same fallacy—Toulmin inserts a short chapter, introductory to the exposition of his own views. This chapter he entitles "Interlude: A Change of Method." Its two short sub-sections bear the simple titles "*Vale...*," "*...et Salve.*"[1]

Traditional moral philosophers and, particularly, those of the twentieth century (against whom the analysts direct most of their critical attacks) are guilty of the same error committed by traditional philosophers in general; they assume that it is their task to provide theoretical explanations of our moral language. Therefore they devote their attention to such questions as "What is the meaning of 'goodness,' 'rightness,' 'moral obligation'?" And so on. Their fallacious attempt to theorize about moral language takes the particular form it does by their commission of another error, which might appropriately be called the "descriptive fallacy." The descriptive fallacy provides a good illustration of the way in which philosophers are bewitched by the grammatical forms of our language. The moral philosophy of G. E. Moore

---

[1] Cf. S. E. Toulmin, *An Examination of the Place of Reason in Ethics* (Cambridge, 1950), pp. 61–64.

is an excellent case in point. According to Moore, the fundamental question of ethics is "What is 'good'?" Now, "good" is an adjective and adjectives, our grammar books tell us, ascribe properties to their subjects. Therefore, "good" must be a property of certain subjects.[1] However, it is not an empirical property, like the color yellow. Rather, we must conclude that "good" is a unique, non-natural property that we apprehend by an act of immediate intuition. But such a non-natural, intuited property is a monstrosity that nobody but a philosopher, carried away by the apparent demands of a theory, would for a moment seriously believe to exist. What led Moore inexorably to his paradoxical conclusion about goodness was the assumption, based on grammatical form, that, since all adjectives ascribe properties to their subjects, "good," being an adjective, must do so too. If he had not been obsessed with the urge to provide a theoretical explanation of our moral language he need never have been led into such an error. And if he had devoted more attention to the way in which we actually use language, he would have seen that we employ adjectives, including "good," for purposes other than description.

This final point gives us the clue to the analysts' views on moral philosophy. We must free ourselves of our theoretical preconceptions and direct our attention to moral language as it is actually used, observing this usage closely and, as philosophers, simply describing as carefully and completely as we can what we find. If we adopt this new point of view, the first thing we become aware of is that the function of moral language is practical rather than descriptive or theoretical. The purpose for which we ordinarily use moral language is not to describe the world but to help people, ourselves and others, to reach decisions. We use it to help us in answering the question "What shall I do?" We can understand our moral words only if we see them in their practical context, against the background of the moral decisions that we must make. Once we realize this, we get an entirely different perspective of moral language. We recognize that, when someone says "Such and such is good," he is not attributing a non-natural property to it at all. Rather he is praising it or commending it. Furthermore, unless he is indulging in idle chatter, he is doing so for a practical reason. The purpose of his commendation is to help himself or someone else reach a decision about what to do. Or, when someone says "You

[1] The fact that Moore calls "good" a "non-descriptive" property, instead of freeing him from the descriptive fallacy, simply gives evidence of the fact that his original commission of the fallacy inevitably led him into further absurdities.

have a moral obligation to keep your promise," he is not burdening you with some strange entity, a moral obligation. Rather he is advising you or exhorting you to keep your promise.

The new approach of the analysts cuts the ground out from under traditional moral philosophy. Its theoretical explanations are seen to be unnecessary for, as Wittgenstein says, "everything lies open to view." All that the moral philosopher has to do is to open his eyes and look—or, perhaps, open his ears and listen—and then describe what he finds. And what he must listen to is the ordinary, unconcealed use of moral language that is going on all around him. This new conception of the task of the moral philosopher is clearly revealed in the subtitle given by P. H. Nowell-Smith to his book *Ethics*: "A Study of the words and concepts that we use for answering practical questions, making decisions, advising, warning, and appraising conduct."[1] Since it is not the function of moral language to describe anything, we might thus define moral philosophy, as the analysts conceive it, as the description of a form of non-descriptive language.

To some the analysts' conception of moral philosophy as the description of ordinary moral language might seem to make the task of the moral philosopher easy. Certainly it is true that he is relieved of one great burden—that of developing and defending complex and sometimes seemingly far-fetched theories of the meaning of moral concepts. But he still has a difficult job to do, one that requires careful research, psychological and verbal sensitivity, and open-mindedness. For our moral discourse is far from easy to describe accurately and adequately. To fulfil our practical purposes we use a great variety of different words and combinations of words in manifold ways and with the finest shadings of difference and most subtle relationships between them. The moral philosopher, if he is to succeed in describing our usage satisfactorily, must taken note of the slightest nuances that appear in it. This is no mean task. But the analytic moral philosophers have devoted a great deal of effort to it, as is readily apparent to anyone familiar with their contributions to the philosophical journals in the past few years. As a result, philosophers today probably know more about the moral language people use and the ways in which they use it than they have ever known before. Naturally, also, in such a difficult and exacting occupation as this differences of opinion are bound to occur. To mention just one illustration, there has been considerable discussion recently of whether our purpose in calling something good

[1] P. H. Nowell-Smith, *Ethics* (London, 1954).

is to *commend* it or to *recommend* it. Needless to say, there is plenty of room within analytic philosophy for the most subtle interpretation and argument. Nor is there much danger, as some critics of the movement have suggested, that the analysts will soon have solved all the questions of moral philosophy and will find themselves left with nothing more to do.

5. ANALYSIS AND THE PROBLEM OF MORAL KNOWLEDGE

The analysts do not all agree with each other on the question of whether moral knowledge is possible. Some believe that we can, by the use of the analytic method, find good reasons for our beliefs that we ought to act in certain ways; others hold that we cannot. This difference of opinion is reflected in two of the most important books on moral philosophy that have been written by analysts, S. E. Toulmin's *The Place of Reason in Ethics* and P. H. Nowell-Smith's *Ethics*. In the final chapter of his book Toulmin concludes that he has provided the best of reasons for our beliefs about what the right thing to do is;[1] Nowell-Smith, on the contrary, writes: "Philosophical arguments ... have no direct bearing on moral questions. From a study of the uses of language no conclusions about what we ought to do can follow..."[2]

The fact that Toulmin and Nowell-Smith disagree on the question of whether analysis can provide a justification for moral knowledge complicates the task of reviewing and evaluating the position itself. However, such complication has its compensations for, by inviting us to seek the reason for their disagreement, it forces us to examine carefully and in some detail the logical structure of the analytic theory. From such an examination we should be able to determine which of the two writers has drawn the implications for moral philosophy demanded by his assumptions and why. We may be enabled also to derive some more general conclusions about the tenability of the analytic approach to philosophy as a whole. It should be reiterated that, although Toulmin and Nowell-Smith disagree on the question of whether our beliefs about our moral obligations can be justified, they are at one in their acceptance of analysis; that is, they both rest their case on the assumption, taken from Wittgenstein, that any conclusion they reach must be derived from a descriptive account of ordinary

---

[1] Cf. S. E. Toulmin, *op. cit.*, p. 224.
[2] P. H. Nowell-Smith, *Ethics* (Oxford, 1957), p. 7. This book, published originally in London in 1954, was republished with a short Preface added. See above, p. 70, n. 1.

language.[1] They differ simply in the results they obtain when they apply the Wittgensteinian thesis to the specific problem of moral knowledge.

Because Toulmin defends the view that moral knowledge is possible and hence rejects skepticism, it is appropriate that I should use his argument in this book. What I shall do is to state his case briefly in this chapter and then, in the first part of the next chapter, try to determine whether it is capable of withstanding the objections of the skeptics. I shall then turn, in the final part of that chapter, to a short discussion of Nowell-Smith, concentrating particularly on the reasons for his differences with Toulmin, and trying to decide whether or in what sense his conclusions are skeptical, and, finally, evaluating these conclusions as an answer to the problem of moral knowledge. (By limiting myself to a discussion of Toulmin and Nowell-Smith I necessarily leave out the writings, some of which are quite important, of several other analytic moral philosophers. In justification of my concentration on these two writers, I should say that their books, in addition to being representative of the movement, are concerned mainly with the problem of moral knowledge, to which their authors, beginning from the same Wittgensteinian assumptions, give quite different solutions.)

As its title indicates, Toulmin's book is concerned with the same general problem that mine is. He begins it, furthermore, in much the same way that I have begun, by asking whether it is possible to give good reasons for the moral decisions we make.

"Which of all these arguments [given in support of a moral decision] should we accept? Which of the reasons are good reasons? And how far can one rely on reason in coming to moral decisions? Is there always a place for reasons and further reasons or does 'giving reasons' sometimes become supererogatory? What, in short, is the place of reason in ethics?"[2]

The first thing we must do, argues Toulmin, is to make clear what people mean by a good reason when they talk about good reasons for moral decision. For not all reasons are good reasons. To be good a reason must be one that is "worthy"[3] of acceptance. Toulmin calls the term, worthy, a *gerundive* concept and draws an analogy between the

---

[1] Cf. S. E. Toulmin, *op. cit.*, pp. 144, 193, 194–195, and P. H. Nowell-Smith, *Ethics* (1957), pp. 56–57, 62, 85–86, 158, 278.

[2] S. E. Toulmin, *op. cit.*, p. 3.

[3] *Ibid.*, p. 71. See his discussion, pp. 70–72; also pp. 121–125.

appeal to gerundives in ethics and in logic and aesthetics. To be valid, an argument must be worthy of acceptance; to be beautiful, a painting must be worthy of admiration; to be right an act must be worthy of approval. Toulmin emphasizes the point that the mere fact that a person accepts a reason as a good one does not make it good. For the person may be mistaken. So in ethics we must carefully distinguish between apparently good reasons and those that are truly good, or really worthy of our acceptance.

Having distinguished between apparently good and really good reasons in ethics Toulmin next turns to the problem of formulating a criterion in terms of which the two can be distinguished. Since this criterion is the heart of his position, he devotes most of his book to its formulation and defense. He begins with the assumption that, to discover the criterion that makes reasons in ethics worthy of acceptance, we must turn our attention to the situations in which people ordinarily give such reasons and see what function these reasons actually perform. We must ask such questions as: When do people ask for or give reasons of this type? Why do they do so? What is the point or purpose of such reasons? By turning his inquiry in this direction Toulmin clearly reflects the influence of Wittgenstein. Traditional moral philosophers, he argues, make the mistake of trying to reduce ethical reasoning to the same type as that used in science, logic, and mathematics. And when they find that their efforts end in failure they are forced into skepticism. But why should anyone think that good reasons in ethics will be of the same kind as good reasons in science, mathematics, or logic? Philosophers have been misled into thinking so by their urge to theorize and by their assumption that the models of theoretical activity are those used in these fields. As a result they have torn ethical reasoning out of its context of use and have tried to force it into a pattern into which it cannot fit, because it is not meant to. Had they stopped to observe how reasoning is actually used in ethics, they would have seen that their efforts were not only vain and misguided but unnecessary as well. Generalizing this point, Toulmin concludes: "... every mode of reasoning, every type of sentence, and (if one is particular) every single sentence will have its own logical criteria, to be discovered by examining its individual, peculiar uses."[1] And this includes ethical reasoning.

If we abandon the futile attempt to theorize and simply observe the way in which reasoning is used in ethics, we see that it always functions

[1] *Ibid.*, p. 83.

in a practical context. People ask for reasons when they are faced with a decision and need guidance in determining which of the alternative courses of action open to them they ought to choose. Our purpose in giving reasons, either to our selves or to others, is to provide such guidance. According to Toulmin the function of ethical judgments is "to alter one's feelings and behavior."[1] But this description of the function of ethical judgments (or reasoning) is incomplete because it does not distinguish ethical judgments from other kinds of judgments that perform the same function, that of influencing our behavior. For example, if someone faced with a choice between two alternative actions asks us "Which should I do?" and we reply "You ought to do A," it is impossible to tell, without further information, whether the "ought" we are using is the moral "ought" at all. For it may very well be the prudential "ought." To complete our account and, hence, to distinguish the moral use of "ought" from other uses of the same word we must discover the purposes that reasons given in favor of practical decisions must be aimed at fulfilling before people are willing to call the reasons moral or ethical.[2] Toulmin's conclusion, derived from an examination of the way in which we actually use the relevant terms, is that the purpose reasons that we call "moral" seek to realize is to "correlate our feelings and behavior in such a way as to make the fulfilment of everyone's aims and desires as far as possible compatible."[3]

The next step in the argument is to establish a criterion in terms of which we can decide what moral reasons are good ones. This turns out to be a simple task. If the function of practical reasons is to influence behavior and the purpose of distinctively moral reasons is to make the fulfilment of everyone's aims and desires as far as possible compatible, then a good moral reason will be one that successfully fulfils its function in the realization of this purpose. That is to say, it will be a reason that influences people to act in such a way that their action contributes to the realization of the purpose stated. To determine the specific moral reasons that are good it is necessary only to discover what reasons do as a matter of fact influence our action in the way

[1] *Ibid.*, p. 130. Toulmin's use of the word "alter" here is a bit puzzling. It seems to suggest that reasons are given in ethics only on occasions in which the agent would feel or act in a way different from that advised unless the reasons were given. This is a restriction on the use of reasoning in ethics that I do not believe Toulmin would himself defend. Later in the same paragraph he states that the function of arguments (or reasoning) in ethics is to *influence* our behavior. This term seems to me to express his meaning more accurately than the restrictive "alter."

[2] Cf. *ibid.*, p. 132.

[3] *Ibid.*, p. 137.

required. We are influenced to act by the reasons we accept; hence the moral philosopher's task is simply to observe and note what reasons we do recognize and accept in reaching our moral decisions and acting on them. Toulmin concludes that these reasons are of two kinds. In the first place we accept as a good reason for the performance of an action the fact that the course of action recommended conforms to the moral code of the community of which the agent is a member.[1] We accept this as a good reason because the moral codes of communities, and the laws and institutions which embody them, are in most instances instruments for achieving the greatest possible fulfilment of the aims and desires of the members of the community as a whole.

Although the appeal to accepted moral practice is the primary method of providing a good reason for moral decisions and action, there are two situations in which it fails. The first of these is one in which no single alternative the agent could choose would uniquely conform to the moral code of his community. When this occurs moral philosophers usually speak of the situation as one in which there is a "conflict of duties." The other case is one in which the moral code of the community itself is either questioned or rejected. If the practices it sanctions fail to serve the purpose of ethics, then people do not offer as a good reason for a decision the fact that the action chosen will conform to the current code. In both kinds of situation—where there is a conflict of duties within the accepted code or where the code itself is not accepted—to provide a good reason for our decisions we turn to the consequences of the alternative actions themselves, choosing as the right act the one whose consequences are least likely to cause suffering to others.[2] Toulmin summarizes his conclusions about the alternative ways in which reasons for a moral decision can, by fulfilling the function of ethics, be defended as good reasons as follows: "If it [the action chosen] is an action which is an unambiguous instance of a maxim generally accepted in the community concerned, it will be right [i.e., we will have a good reason for doing it] just because it *is* an instance of such a maxim; but, if it is an action over which there is a 'conflict of duties,' or is itself a principle (or social practice) as opposed to a particular action, it will be right or wrong accordingly as its consequences are likely to be good or bad."[3] For Toulmin the appeal to a socially sanctioned principle or practice is the primary test that we

[1] Cf. *ibid.*, pp. 144–146 and p. 223.
[2] Cf. *ibid.*, pp. 140–143 and 146–150.
[3] *Ibid.*, p. 154.

apply (or the first appeal that we make) in justifying an action; however, in cases where this appeal fails, our final justification is always in terms of consequences.[1] And these reasons, given in justification of moral decisions, are good reasons because they are the reasons that people do, in the practical affairs of life, accept and act on. Toulmin is not intending, in other words, to propose a moral *theory* whose purpose is to justify a certain type of moral reasons. Rather he believes himself simply to be describing, in the analysts' fashion, the use of moral language that he actually observes, taking special note of the occasions on which people use such language, the purposes for which they employ it, and the criteria they use in judging it.

[1] Cf. *ibid.*, p. 147.

CHAPTER V

DUTY AND ORDINARY LANGUAGE

In the last chapter of *The Place of Reason in Ethics* Toulmin gives the following summary statement of his conclusions:

"Of course, 'This practice would involve the least conflict of interests attainable under the circumstances' does not *mean* the same as 'This would be the right practice'; nor does 'This way of life would be more harmoniously satisfying' *mean* the same as 'This would be better.' But in each case, the first statement is *a good reason* for the second: the 'ethically neutral' fact is *a good reason* for the 'gerundive' moral judgment. If the adoption of the practice would genuinely reduce conflicts of interest, it is a practice *worthy of adoption*, and if the way of life would genuinely lead to a deeper and more consistent happiness, it is one *worthy of pursuit*. And this seems so natural and intelligible, when one bears in mind the function of ethical judgments, that, if anyone asks me *why* they are 'good reasons,' I can only reply by asking in return 'What better kinds of reason could you want?'"[1]

My object in the first part of this chapter will be to determine whether the reasons that Toulmin gives really are, as he holds them to be, *good* reasons. To do this I shall have to analyze and evaluate the argument on which his conclusion rests. Before I begin this job, however, I should make more clear than I did in the last chapter exactly how Toulmin's analytic theory differs from traditional methods of solving the problem of moral knowledge. Such a clarification of his theory is particularly necessary because his conclusion, which I have just quoted, can easily be, and has been, interpreted in a way that places him among the ranks, not of the analysts, but of traditional moral philosophers.

1. AN INTERPRETATION OF TOULMIN'S CONCLUSIONS

In a review of *The Place of Reason in Ethics* C. D. Broad summarizes the conclusions Toulmin reaches concerning good reasons for moral

[1] S. E. Toulmin, *An Examination of the Place of Reason in Ethics*, p. 224.

decisions and then makes the following comment: "It would appear from the above that Mr. Toulmin's answer to his question ['What kind of factual premises are valid reasons for moral conclusions?'] is a form of a very old and highly respectable ethical theory, *viz.*, hedonistic utilitarianism."[1] If Broad is correct in his interpretation of Toulmin's theory—and he is a person whose judgment in such matters always deserves serious consideration—then my contention that Toulmin is a revolutionary thinker who makes a decisive break with traditional moral philosophy is simply mistaken. Yet I have cited evidence (in 4.4) that Toulmin himself, in the early part of his book, did consider himself to be doing just what I have said he did. Has something happened in the course of the book which has led him finally back into the traditional camp or does he end, Broad to the contrary, with a solution to the problem of moral knowledge as radically different from the tradition as he promised to do in the beginning? If the second alternative is correct, as I shall argue that it is, then Broad has misunderstood him. To decide the issue, and at the same time to determine just what Toulmin's view is, it will be necessary to examine at some length his summary statement that I have cited above, looking at it both in itself and in relation to the argument that leads up to it.

The quotation, unfortunately, is not altogether clear. As simply a short concluding statement recapitulating the main argument of the book, it does not pretend to be either complete or tightly organized logically. Nevertheless, the main point that Toulmin is making in it seems to be obvious enough. What he appears to be doing is to be summarizing his answer to the question "Why ought one to do acts of a certain type?" And he answers this question by an appeal to the goodness of the consequences of acts of the type in question, interpreting "goodness" in an apparently hedonistic way, by such phrases as "harmoniously satisfying" and "deeper and more consistent happiness." Thus his position seems to be just what Broad characterized it as—a form of hedonistic utilitarianism. If it is not that, then, to say the least, its appearance is deceptive. Given the text as it stands (as well as other statements that appear in the course of the argument), it seems to me that Broad has provided a plausible interpretation of Toulmin's position. If, as I am contending, this interpretation is radically mistaken, Toulmin can legitimately be criticized for being obscure. For anyone who writes in such a way that Broad fails to get his point

[1] C. D. Broad, "Review of Toulmin: *An Examination of the Place of Reason in Ethics*," *Mind*, N.S.—61 (1952), 94, 93.

is seriously lacking in the ability to communicate. In Toulmin's defense, however, I think it must be said that a part of the reason why Broad failed to grasp his point is that his view is *so* revolutionary that Broad, accustomed to reasoning in traditional ways, just failed to take note of the verbally insignificant, but theoretically crucial, differences between what Toulmin actually says in his conclusion and what a hedonistic utilitarian would have said. Just what are these differences and why do they distinguish Toulmin's theory sharply from traditional hedonism? This is what I must now try to show.

2. A REINTERPRETATION OF TOULMIN'S CONCLUSIONS

If a hedonistic utilitarian is asked "Why ought one to do a certain act?" (or "What is a good reason for believing that one ought to do it?"), he will reply "One ought to do it because its performance will produce the greatest possible amount of pleasure." If he is then asked "Why is the fact that an act will produce the greatest possible amount of pleasure a good reason for believing that one ought to do it?" he will reply "Because pleasure is good in itself, in fact the only thing good in itself." If one then goes on to ask him "But why ought one to act in such a way as to produce the most possible *good*?" he will have no answer to give. As a utilitarian, he cannot answer this question because it asks him to provide a justification for the very criterion of duty which his theory sets up. To provide such a justification he would have to appeal to something other than the goodness of consequences. Thus he would have to seek a further criterion of duty, outside of his utilitarian theory. If he were to do this, he would, in effect, be denying that his appeal to the goodness of consequences is really ultimate, hence would be denying that it is the ground on which he bases his conclusions about the acts we ought to do. In other words, he would be giving up the utilitarian theory. As long as one remains a utilitarian, therefore, he must reject any attempt to question the appeal to the goodness of its consequences as an adequate and final reason for judging an act to be a duty.

If Toulmin is a hedonistic utilitarian, then he must end his attempts to justify our duties at the point I have just indicated. Does he do so? To answer this question let us follow the steps that he would go through in defending an assertion of the type "One ought to do act X." In the first place, he would argue that one ought to do act X if act X conforms to the accepted moral code of the community in which he lives. There

are two kinds of situations, however, in which the appeal to accepted
social practice does not provide a good reason for deciding an act to
be one's duty. If someone asks "Ought I to do act X?" and either (1)
there is an incompatible, alternative act Y which conforms equally to
the moral code of the community or (2) the general practice of which
X is an example, although sanctioned by the accepted code, does not
contribute to the greatest harmony of individual aims and desires, then
one cannot answer by appealing to what is demanded by the established
code. Instead he will have to base his answer on an appeal to the
relative goodness of the consequences of act X or any possible alternative act, advising the person that his duty is to do the act whose
consequences are the best possible. If we give the notion of "good
consequences" a hedonistic interpretation, as Toulmin does, then we
seem to end with hedonistic utilitarianism, *if* this is the final appeal
that Toulmin can make in justifying any assertion about duty. So the
question we must now raise is this: If we were to ask Toulmin *why* we
ought to do the act whose consequences are the best possible, would
he, on his theory, be able to give us any answer? If so, what would it be?

The clue to Toulmin's reply to these questions is contained in a
clause that appears in the last sentence of the quotation that I cited
at the beginning of the chapter, "when one bears in mind the function
of ethical judgments." Because it is embedded in a context that reads
like an affirmation of traditional hedonistic utilitarianism, this clause
is easily overlooked—as it was, presumably, by Broad. Yet it states
a condition that no traditional moral philosopher, hedonist or otherwise, would insert into a summary of his theory. On the contrary, it is
his insertion of this qualification into his statement that marks the
crucial difference between Toulmin's view and any traditional theory
of moral knowledge. To understand the logic of Toulmin's position we
must begin with this clause, because it provides the key that opens
the way into the analytic theory of moral obligation. As he implies in
the quotation, his explanation of why a reason given in favor of an
ethical judgment is a good reason turns on his view of the function of
such judgments. What, then, is the function of ethical judgments and
how does this function enable us to decide which of the reasons given
in favor of ethical judgments are good ones?

According to Toulmin the function of ethical judgments is "to correlate our feelings and behavior in such a way as to make the fulfilment
of everyone's aims and desires as far as possible compatible."[1] This

---

[1] S. E. Toulmin, *op. cit.*, p. 137 and sqq.

statement is descriptive rather than theoretical. It is a generalization Toulmin has derived from his observation of the way in which people actually use moral language in the ordinary affairs of life and of the purpose for which they use it. Having stated the purpose for which ethical reasons are given, it would seem that as the next step in the logic of his argument Toulmin would go on (in good Aristotelian style) to distinguish good reasons as those which successfully fulfil this purpose. Although he nowhere formulates this step explicitly, it fairly clearly forms a part of his argument and is implied by the structure of the reasoning that does appear in his book.[1] Probably he assumed it to be so obvious as not to need explicit statement.

But what kinds of reasons given in support of a moral judgment are, because they lead to the most compatible fulfilment of everyone's aims and desires, good reasons? Toulmin's first answer is: Reasons which show that the action recommended falls within a class of actions supported by the moral code of the community of which the agent is a member. As he puts it:

"Ethics is concerned with the harmonious satisfaction of desires and interests. On most occasions it is a good reason for choosing or approving of an action that it is in accordance with an established maxim of conduct, *for* the existing moral code, and the current institutions and laws, provide the most reliable guide as to which decision will be happy..."[2]

On some occasions, however, appeal to the accepted code does not give a good reason for action. When there is either a "conflict of duties" or the code itself is inimical to social harmony, we must look elsewhere for our moral justifications. Then, Toulmin believes, the appeal must be to the relative goodness of the consequences of the contemplated actions. Although he leaves this point somewhat obscure, what he apparently means by "good consequences" is states of affairs in which the greatest harmony among individual interests and desires is realized.[3]

---

[1] In his explanation of the logic of scientific reasoning, which he holds to be analogous, in its structure, to ethical reasoning, Toulmin explicitly includes this step in his account, maintaining that the function of scientific theories (reasons or explanations) is to predict our future experiences and that a good theory is one that succeeds in fulfilling this function. Cf. *ibid.*, Chapter 7, esp. pp. 88, 95, and 101. However, this does not provide the logically final reason, either in science or in ethics, for calling a theory or reason good.

[2] *Ibid.*, p. 223. Italics mine. If we assume that Toulmin means by "happy" decisions those that will further the "harmonious satisfaction of desires and interests," it is clear that the argument of this passage implies the step that I have inserted into his argument above, that a good reason in ethics is one that fulfils successfully the function for which such reasons are given.

[3] Cf. *ibid.*, pp. 137, 142–143, and 149–150.

In other words, when it is impossible to justify an action by appeal to the established code, we must appeal directly to the purpose for which ethical reasons are given.

We have now, it would appear, given Toulmin's answer to the question, Why ought we to do the act with the best consequences? This is that the reason that an act will have the best possible consequences, given as a reason for doing the act, successfully fulfils the function for which ethical reasons are given, which is to promote social harmony. By giving this answer Toulmin distinguishes himself from the traditional utilitarians. For he has not reached the end of his process of ethical justification when he establishes that a given act will produce the best possible consequences, as have the utilitarians. Rather he goes a step further, justifying the appeal to good consequences as a good reason for moral action in terms of its success in fulfilling the function for which such reasons are given.

The distinction I have just tried to draw between Toulmin's theory of ethical justification and that of traditional utilitarianism may seem both unclear and unimportant. The crucial point, that can easily be lost sight of, is that Toulmin's reason for holding that the goodness of its consequences renders an act our duty is not that he accepts (what the hedonists do accept) the harmonious satisfaction of individual desires and interests as an ultimate ethical end. Social harmony is an end, and thus can justify our moral judgments, only because people accept it as such, hence make its fullest realization their purpose in giving ethical reasons. It would be possible, consistently with his theory, for Toulmin to maintain that a good reason in ethics is one that successfully fulfils the function for which such reasons are given and at the same time deny that its harmonious satisfaction of desires and interests is a good reason for doing an act. This would be true in a situation in which people did not use moral reasons to perform that function, a fact which Toulmin, as a moral philosopher, would simply observe and describe. At this point, thus, Toulmin's theory departs sharply from hedonistic utilitarianism. For the hedonist, it is the intrinsic nature of goodness (interpreted as pleasure) that makes its production the justification for our judgments of moral action; for Toulmin the fact that the end of social harmony justifies our moral judgments has nothing to do with the intrinsic goodness of social harmony but rests simply on the contingent fact, which he has observed, that people *do* accept the appeal to social harmony as a good reason for moral action, and act accordingly. Thus, Toulmin holds that the final justification for the view that a good reason is one that promotes social harmony is that it is the reason which people do as a matter of fact accept. Only because people do use reasons in ethics to further social harmony are reasons which successfully serve this purpose good reasons. Toulmin, himself, summarizes his conclusion in the following way:

"So far, however, I have not given an explicit answer to the question from which we set out: namely, 'What is it, in an ethical discussion, that makes a reason a good reason, or an argument a valid argument?'..."

In this chapter, I have not attempted to give a 'theory of ethics'; I have simply tried to describe the occasions on which we are in fact prepared to call judgments 'ethical' and decisions 'moral' and the part which reasoning plays on such occasions. This description has led us to see how, in *particular types* of ethical question and argument, good reasoning is distinguished from bad, and valid argument from invalid—to be specific, by applying to individual judgments the test of principle, and to principles the test of general fecundity.

Now we have to ask, 'Is any further answer [to the question he has asked in the first paragraph of the quotation] needed? Given particular rules applicable to different kinds of ethical judgment and question, have we not all we want? And, if any more were needed, could it not be supplied from an account, more detailed and accurate than has been given, but of the same kind?"[1]

3. GOOD REASONS AND GENERALLY ACCEPTED REASONS

In the last paragraph of the above quotation, Toulmin makes it clear that for him there is no need to seek a justification for reasons in ethics beyond those that people actually give and accept. Once we have discovered, by the kind of observation that he has employed (only perhaps more detailed and accurate), what reasons for action people do, in their everyday moral affairs, accept as good reasons, we have all the answer anyone can require to the question: What reasons for moral action are good reasons?

---

[1] *Ibid.*, pp. 160–161. It should be noted that Toulmin's summary statement here is descriptive throughout and that he explicitly disavows the formulation of an explanatory theory. His statement, in the second paragraph, "This description has led us to see how... good reasoning *is* (italics mine) distinguished from bad..." is critical to his theory. It implies that for him a good reason in ethics is one that is, in practice, generally accepted as a good reason.

Is Toulmin's position tenable? Before attempting to answer this question, I should like to consider, briefly (and from a slightly different perspective), the reasoning that led him to it. The conclusion Toulmin has reached is the logical outcome of the methodology he has employed. If the function of the philosopher is to describe as accurately as possible the way in which people actually use various linguistic expressions, then the conclusions that he reaches can be nothing but descriptive generalizations derived from his observations, which must be judged according to the fidelity and adequacy with which they reflect ordinary usage. The fatal error, which the philosopher must avoid at all costs, is the attempt to criticize, judge, or justify ordinary usage. In Wittgenstein's words: "Philosophy may in no way interfere with the actual use of language; it can in the end only describe it. For it cannot give it any foundation either."[1] What Toulmin has done in his book is to apply this Wittgensteinian dictum to the specific problem of moral knowledge. The question with which he began was: What reasons given in justification of moral action are good reasons? And his answer is: Those reasons which people accept as good reasons *are* good reasons. They are good because they are generally called good.

In giving this answer Toulmin is simply working out the implications of his ordinary language assumptions. The logic of his argument thus is quite straightforward. That his theory, as he develops it at length in his book, is an elaboration of the simple structure I have just presented can be shown as follows: The reason why "Act X will promote social harmony" is a good reason for "One has a duty to do act X" is that this reason successfully fulfils the function for which ethical reasons are given, this function being the promotion of social harmony. (The same, of course, holds true, with the necessary qualifications, of "Act X conforms to the established moral code.") But why does "Act X will promote social harmony," given as a reason for doing act X, actually succeed in promoting social harmony? Toulmin's answer is: It gets act X done. Therefore, since X is an act of a kind whose performance will promote social harmony, getting it done furthers that end. But why does giving "Act X will promote social harmony" as a reason for doing act X get X done? The reason, Toulmin would say, is that people in general accept this as a good reason for doing the act and therefore act accordingly. To the further question "Why do people in general accept this reason as a good reason?" Toulmin does not, as far as I know, provide any definitive answer. I think he would say that the

[1] L. Wittgenstein, *Philosophical Investigations*, § 124.

detailed investigation of such a point is outside of his province as a philosopher. To find answers to questions of that type is the responsibility of the historians, anthropologists, and psychologists. (He might, stepping out of his strictly philosophical role, essay the answer that people in general desire social harmony.) As far as ethics is concerned, the question is irrelevant. Whatever motivates people to accept as good reasons the reasons that they do, the fact remains that they do accept certain reasons and act accordingly. It is the task of the moral philosopher to describe what these reasons are, as he finds them being used, for by being generally accepted, they are made good reasons, hence provide a moral justification for action.

To summarize Toulmin's position, then, he holds that certain reasons given in ethics are good reasons on the following two (closely interrelated) grounds: (1) Because they successfully fulfil the function for which such reasons are given and (2) because they are generally accepted as good reasons. Admitting their complex relationships with each other, how can these two justifications be distinguished in Toulmin's theory? The first justification is psychological. It gives Toulmin's explanation of why people do accept the reasons in question as good reasons. Because they use reasoning in their practical affairs for a specific purpose, they accept as good those reasons which lead to a fulfilment of that purpose. The second justification is logical or theoretical. Whatever the reasons people may in fact accept as good reasons (something for the philosopher to discover by observation and the psychologist to attempt to explain fully), the goodness of those reasons lies in their being accepted as such. Needless to say, it is Toulmin's second justification that expresses his final analytic solution to the problem of moral knowledge. To put the point briefly, Toulmin's first justification could be said to explain why people *call* the reasons in question good reasons and the second to explain why they *are* good reasons.

4 TOULMIN'S THEORY AND THE DEDUCTIVE FALLACY

What would a moral skeptic say to all this? "You are asking me," he might well retort to Toulmin, "to recognize a duty to do a certain act because members of my society have accepted the act as their duty. But I couldn't care less what they accept. If you are to convince *me*, you must present some argument that will show me that *I* ought to do the act. As for your contention that the purpose people have in view in accepting certain acts as their duties is the promotion of social harmony, two comments seem in order: (1) You have made the existence of duties contingent on our purposes, so, if we may assume that our purposes reflect our wants, needs, and desires, you have broken down the distinction between obligation and inclination, subordinating the former to the latter. Furthermore, (2) because of its appeal to the end of social harmony, your argument for duty has weight only with someone who shares that end. But I do not; I am interested only in my own welfare, an end that I can attain quite successfully by my own efforts. I do not ask others to defer to my welfare nor am I prepared to defer to theirs. I can take care of myself; I expect others to do the same. Therefore I recognize no duties to them." So much for the objections of an extremely individualistic egoist. A more enlightened egoist might take up the cudgels against Toulmin with the following argument: "I accept the end of social harmony and am willing to act accordingly. However, I do not accept it as an end-in-itself but only as a necessary means to the real end, my own greatest well-being. Thus, the actions that you characterize as duties, I call stratagems. I desire to be happy and I realize that I can gain this end only in a society in which others are happy too. So I am willing to make the sacrifices necessary for the fulfilment of my desire. To do this, however, is not to recognize any moral obligation to my fellows but only to do what has to be done in order to get what I want."

How might Toulmin respond to criticisms like these? One could answer such a question better if he had devoted more of his book to a sustained defense of his case against the stock arguments available to the skeptics. Although he raises and answers skeptical objections sporadically in the course of his text, he tends to brush critics aside with rhetoric, for example asking—as he does in the summary quotation with which I began this chapter—"... if anyone asks me *why* they are 'good reasons,' I can only reply by asking in return, 'What better kinds of reason could you want?'" But surely the skeptic *does* want better kinds of reasons than Toulmin has given. Toulmin is quite aware of this fact for he writes earlier in his book: "...I recall a conversation with Bertrand Russell in which he remarked, as an objection to the present account of Ethics, that it would not have convinced Hitler. But who ever supposed that it should? We do not prescribe logic as a treatment for lunacy, or expect philosophers to produce panaceas for psychopaths."[1] Assuming that Toulmin did not miss the

[1] S. E. Toulmin, *op. cit.*, p. 165, n. 2.

point of Russell's objection, his answer is certainly a good one. For no theory should be judged by the impression it makes on lunatics. Nevertheless, it is no reply to the moral skeptic, who rejects Toulmin's theory, not because he is a psychopath (which he is not), but because he fails to find the arguments that Toulmin has marshalled in its favor at all convincing. It is on this point—on the logic of his argument rather than on any appeal to rhetoric, either pro or con—that our evaluation of Toulmin's theory must rest. So, instead of pursuing the various skeptical objections we have just raised any further, let us turn directly to the logical structure of Toulmin's theory to see if it will bear critical scrutiny.

As should be apparent from what I have said already, Toulmin's argument in justification of the thesis that certain reasons given in ethics are good reasons can be cast into simple syllogistic form, as follows:

People generally accept certain reasons for doing an action as good reasons.

Reason X (*e.g.*, that the action will promote social harmony) is a reason that is so accepted.

Therefore, X is a good reason for doing the action.

Or, to translate Toulmin's "good reasons" into traditional moral terminology:

People generally accept certain acts to be their duty.

Act X is an act that is so accepted.

Therefore, we have a duty (or ought) to do act X.

It may hardly seem necessary, at this stage in the proceedings, to criticize Toulmin's argument. One has only to read through the syllogisms to realize, without need for further comment, that the conclusions do not follow logically from the premises. Toulmin has, in fact, blatantly committed the deductive fallacy. From purely factual or descriptive premises he has attempted to deduce "gerundive" conclusions. Or, put in the language we have been using, his mistake lies in his attempt to deduce an "ought" from an "is." In attempting to do this he falls into the same trap in which Hume found his contemporaries floundering.

Here, however, someone may object, arguing on Toulmin's behalf that my criticism rests on a misapprehension of his position. For Toulmin makes it quite clear, as I have myself already admitted (in

4.5), that it is not enough, to render a reason given in ethics a good reason, for it to be in fact accepted as good. In addition, it must be *worthy* of acceptance. As he makes the distinction:

"I have analyzed at length the 'subjective' approach to ethics, which attempts to account for ethical concepts in terms of the attitudes of the speaker and hearer alone, and shown that it is fallacious. If we are to conclude that some past deed was 'good' or that some proposed course of action is 'right,' it is not enough for us to know that we ourselves are psychologically disposed to approve of the deed, or that the proposed course seems right to the agent: we must have reasons for thinking that the act was *worthy of* approval, or that the course of action is *worthy of* selection."[1]

This objection calls for several comments. It must be agreed that Toulmin distinguishes his position from that held by traditional subjectivists. As he says, he does not believe that an act is made worthy of approval simply by being approved of by "the speaker and hearer alone," or by "the agent," as the subjectivists do. It does not follow from this, however, that Toulmin does not believe that an act can be made worthy of approval by being approved of by *someone*. It has been my contention, based on an analysis of his argument as he develops it in the course of his book, that Toulmin accepts the view that the "gerundive" conclusion that an act is "worthy of approval" is derivable from the "ethically neutral" fact that it is approved of by the society in which it is performed—their approval being motivated by the fact that performance of the act contributes to the purpose for which they give moral approvals, namely, the achievement of social harmony. Without here going to the length of recapitulating Toulmin's argument, I should like nevertheless to note two important statements that he makes on the subject of the grounds on which he holds that gerundive moral conclusions can be based. In the opening paragraph of Chapter 11, which is entitled "The Logic of Moral Reasoning," he writes, "The only facts, upon which the truth of what we have to say will depend, are those more familiar, unquestionable facts of usage... namely, facts about the ways in which *we* do recognize a 'duty,' a 'community' and so on."[2] The second "we," which I have italicized, has to be understood, in this context, as the communal "we"; Toulmin means by this "we" people in general. Hence, what he is implying by this statement is that the conclusions which he will reach about what

---

[1] *Ibid.*, p. 71.
[2] *Ibid.*, p. 144. Italics mine.

our duties are (or what acts are worthy of approval) will rest on the facts he discovers about acts people in general recognize as duties (or approve of). Later, in a summary statement, he makes the same general point in slightly different terms:

"As soon as the truth of this [that traditional ethical theories can teach us nothing] is recognized, the desire for a theory vanishes. A *descriptive* account of our ethical concepts is what we need; a less cursory one than I have given, perhaps, but a descriptive account nevertheless. ... It will be from such a description, or 'language-map,' rather than from a one-sided and disguised comparison, that we shall obtain the understanding we seek of what it is that makes an ethical argument a valid argument, and what things are *good reasons* for ethical judgments."[1]

In this summary statement Toulmin reiterates the Wittgensteinian thesis that the function of philosophy is not to theorize but simply to describe. If our goal is to discover what reasons given in support of an ethical judgment are good reasons, we must avoid the traditional attempt to develop some theory which will allegedly answer our question and devote our attention instead to an observation of the reasons that people do as a matter of fact give, taking special note of those reasons that, when given, are accepted as good reasons. Now, if the conclusions we reach as philosophers about good reasons in ethics are based on an observation and description of general usage, then these conclusions, to be correct, must accurately reflect that usage. That is to say, we must accept as good reasons those reasons that people, in their ordinary moral discussions, call good reasons. If we do not do so, our conclusions, because they are not descriptive of ordinary usage, will be in error.

Thus the hypothetical reply I have made on Toulmin's behalf against my criticism of his theory is irrelevant because it misses the real point. The reason why Toulmin is not a subjectivist is not that he rejects the derivation of our duties from what we hold to be our duties but that he rejects the entire traditional approach to the problem of moral knowledge assumed by the subjectivists. In my criticism of his theory I have not raised the issue of a possible similarity between it and subjectivism. Rather, my point is a logical one. I am objecting to his derivation of our duties from what people hold to be our duties not because it renders the notion of duty "subjective" but because it commits the deductive fallacy. Furthermore, the fault in his theory

[1] *Ibid.*, pp. 194–195.

does not lie in the specific nature of the factual or descriptive premises from which he derives his gerundive conclusions but rather in the general fact that he derives such conclusions from factual premises. His argument would remain fallacious no matter what the nature of his premises might be, as long as they were wholly factual or descriptive.

Here, however, a question must be raised. As I said at the time, Toulmin's argument involves a *blatant* commission of the deductive fallacy. I think my use of this adjective was fully justified. When his argument is formalized, nothing could be more clear than the fact that it attempts to derive an "ought" from an "is." So the question arises, How could Toulmin have done this? How could he have permitted the publication of a view resting on such an obvious and logically fundamental error? It could not have been from ignorance; no one acquainted with the ethical writings of Hume and Prichard, as Toulmin obviously is, could have been unaware that his theory lays itself open to the criticism I have made. The only way that we can explain his action is to assume that he committed the fallacy *deliberately*. This assumption, although it may at first blush seem strange, is corroborated as correct by Toulmin himself. Going back once again to the original summary statement quoted at the beginning of the chapter, we find him writing: "But in each case, the first statement is *a good reason* for the second: the 'ethically neutral' fact is *a good reason* for the 'gerundive' moral judgment." Toulmin is, thus, intentionally asserting that it is legitimate to derive gerundive conclusions from factual premises or, in other words, to deduce an "ought" from an "is." He is deliberately maintaining a position that commits the deductive fallacy. But why should he do that? The answer, which probably is apparent by now, is that he does not think that his procedure is fallacious. For Toulmin, what I have termed the deductive fallacy is no fallacy at all.

5. DOES TOULMIN ESCAPE THE DEDUCTIVE FALLACY?

Toulmin's rejection of the deductive fallacy gives the discussion a completely new turn. From the beginning of this book I have been operating on the assumption that the reasons we give for our beliefs about what we ought to do, if they are to qualify as good reasons, must logically imply those beliefs. By challenging this assumption, Toulmin has undercut the entire case that I have developed so far. If he is correct, then much of what I have written up to now can be descarded without ado. However, I can hardly resent that—since the reason for discarding it will be that the problem of moral knowledge has been solved and the moral skeptics successfully answered. So we must try to see if Toulmin is right. In particular we must decide whether he can answer to our satisfaction the question: *Why* are the reasons for moral action that he claims to be good reasons really good reasons? Since Toulmin does not deal with this question in detail in *The Place of Reason in Ethics*, we must turn for his answer to another of his books, *The Uses of Argument*.[1] In this book Toulmin attacks, in a quite general way, the traditionally-accepted philosophical view that, for any conclusion validly to follow from a set of premises, that conclusion must be logically entailed by, or be logically deducible from, those premises. Although such a requirement of logical deducibility may be legitimate in the fields of logic and mathematics, in which the arguments employed are "analytic," it is not applicable in other fields (including ethics), in which the arguments used, and the conclusions reached are "substantial." In support of his attack Toulmin marshalls many ingenious and telling arguments against the traditional position.

It is outside of the scope of the present discussion either to elaborate or to examine critically Toulmin's case against the traditional ideal of deductive entailment as a criterion of argumentative cogency. Instead, what I shall do is to concentrate on Toulmin's proposed analytic position, in the attempt to decide whether it offers a satisfactory alternative to the traditional "deductive" requirement which I have hitherto been accepting. Although Toulmin makes only brief references to the problem of moral knowledge in *The Uses of Argument*, he emphasizes the point that arguments in which we reach moral conclusions are of the "substantial" type, to which the criterion of deductive rigor is inapplicable.[2] But what criterion is applicable? How are we to determine what reasons given in support of a moral conclusion are good reasons? We already know, from our earlier discussion, what reasons given in the moral field Toulmin believes to be good reasons. We must now try to discover the reason why these are good reasons. Or, to put the point in other words, we are asking Toulmin to justify his contention that they are good reasons. He has made a claim; now can he make it good?

---

[1] S. E. Toulmin, *The Uses of Argument* (Cambridge, 1958). Most of the exposition that follows will be based on this book; however I shall not footnote my references to it in any detail.

[2] Cf. *ibid.*, pp. 174–176, 217–223, and 232–235.

Perhaps the best way to start our inquiry is to look again at an argument leading, in Toulmin's view, to a reasonable or valid conclusion about what we ought to do.

People generally accept it to be their duty to act in such a way as to promote social harmony.

Performance of act X will promote social harmony.

Therefore, we have a duty to do act X.

Now it is admitted all around that the conclusion of this argument does not follow deductively from its premises. Yet Toulmin holds that it does follow legitimately from them. To use his own terminology, the major premise gives us a "warrant" for moving from the factual assertion contained in the minor premise to the assertion of obligation contained in the conclusion. To judge whether his view is acceptable, what we must do, therefore, is to decide whether the major premise can legitimately warrant us in drawing the conclusion given.

At this point a skeptical critic might find himself becoming impatient. "Just look at the argument," he might say. "It is obvious that the conclusion does not follow from the premises. I can admit both premises to be true and yet still deny the truth of the conclusion. Under these circumstances what can Toulmin possibly mean by asserting that the conclusion follows legitimately from the premises?" This is, roughly, the response of at least one moral philosopher to Toulmin's theory. In a review of *The Place of Reason in Ethics*, R. M. Hare concludes, ironically: "... what logic cannot do, Mr. Toulmin can, namely infer a moral conclusion without having a moral premise."[1] Although we may sympathize with Hare's criticism, I think we must recognize that it does not constitute any refutation of Toulmin's view. Rather, it begs the question. For Toulmin readily grants that his conclusion does not follow logically (deductively) from his premises. To imply that the conclusion therefore does not follow at all is to assume that the only legitimate method for deriving a conclusion from a set of premises is by means of deductive entailment. But this is just what Toulmin denies.

If we are to come to grips with Toulmin we cannot simply reiterate the point that the major premise of his argument *cannot* serve as a warrant permitting us legitimately to draw his conclusion. Rather, we must be willing to set aside our traditional logical biases and at least

[1] R. M. Hare, "Review of *An Examination of the Place of Reason in Ethics*," *The Philosophical Quarterly*, 1 (1951), 374.

permit him the opportunity to justify his thesis. Let us, then, put our question to him in this way: *Why* does the major premise warrant us in drawing the conclusion?

In reply Toulmin might point out that the logic involved in his argument is simply an application of his general theory to the specific field of morality. Since the task of philosophy is the description of ordinary language, we shall have found the answer to our philosophical problems when we have accurately and adequately described the way in which people ordinarily use the words which have given rise to our original philosophical perplexity. In the case under consideration, we are trying to solve the problem of moral knowledge by finding good reasons for our beliefs about what we ought to do. The problem is solved and moral knowledge vindicated when we make clear the reasons which people do as a matter of fact accept as good reasons. We ought to act in a way that will promote social harmony because people ordinarily believe—and embody this belief in their moral discourse—that we ought to do so. The descriptive statement of what people ordinarily accept warrants us in reaching our normative conclusion because all philosophical conclusions are, and must be, derivable from descriptive accounts of ordinary language.

Such a reply answers our question only by raising it again in a wider context. For what we were asking Toulmin to justify was his contention that ordinary usage in moral matters provides a warrant for a philosophical conclusion about our duty. His answer to this question still leaves unanswered the question of how to provide a justification for the contention that ordinary usage *in general* provides a warrant for philosophical conclusions. How would Toulmin answer the critic who calls into question his appeal to ordinary language as a criterion of philosophical truth altogether? Why should we accept the thesis that we can solve our philosophical problems by discovering how people ordinarily use language, and, in particular, that we can solve the problem of moral knowledge by finding out how they use words like "right" and "duty"? To repeat a passage that I quoted from Toulmin earlier in the chapter, why should we accept his thesis that "the only facts, upon which the truth of what we have to say will depend, are those more familiar, unquestionable facts of usage... namely, facts about the ways in which we do recognize a 'duty,' a 'community' and so on"?

Toulmin would have to reject all of these questions as illegitimate. For if he were to answer them, he would have to find some criterion capable of justifying his entire analytic position. He could not appeal to ordinary usage again, since that would be question-begging, so he would have to go outside the limits of his ordinary language position altogether. But that would be tantamount to abandoning analysis. At this point Toulmin's process of justification has reached the end of its road; we cannot push him further. But where does that leave us? We seem to be at an impasse. Either we accept or reject Toulmin's analytic position, but in any case we do so arbitrarily, because we cannot justify the choice we make without begging the question one way or the other.

Fortunately, I do not think the situation is so desperate as it seems. For the point at issue *can* be settled. To resolve the question, let us begin by taking a slightly different tack. We shall leave open the possibility (which Hare did not) that Toulmin is right, but, on the other hand, we shall not assume that he is right. In other words, we shall avoid begging the question either way at the outset. Approaching the problem of moral knowledge in this neutral way, let us return to the disputed syllogism (on p. 92). Both sides agree that the conclusion does not follow logically from the premises but Toulmin contends that it follows legitimately from them because the major premise warrants our drawing it. Let us assume with him that the conclusion does follow legitimately from the premises. We have already agreed that it does not follow logically from them and we have agreed as well that we shall not assume the truth of his own analytic theory (leaving that question open). If we accept these assumptions it follows that we can replace the major premise of our original syllogism with some other, which will equally legitimately warrant the same conclusion. We can, for example, argue as follows:

> One act that I can do will produce better consequences than any other possible alternative.
>
> Act X is the act in question.
>
> Therefore, I ought to do act X.

In this argument we have not assumed the truth of Toulmin's analytic theory but we have assumed with him that a conclusion can follow legitimately from its premises even though it does not follow logically from them. Our result is the rehabilitation of utilitarianism as a theory of moral obligation. Of course, the conclusion does not follow logically from the premises. But that does not matter. Or we might make our major premise read "God commands us to perform certain acts" and have a vindication of morality based on revelation. And so on. Really it is very easy to refute the moral skeptics.

But our method has certain consequences, too. Let us take the original syllogism and alter it as follows:

People generally accept it to be their duty to act in such a way as to promote social harmony.

Performance of act X will promote social harmony.

Therefore, we have a duty *not* to do act X.

Once again, the conclusion, although it does not follow logically from the premises, does follow from them equally as legitimately as the original conclusion, because *any* conclusion follows equally legitimately from a given set of premises once the requirement of deductive rigor is given up. (It must be remembered that we are not now assuming the truth of Toulmin's analytic theory.) But this new conclusion contradicts the conclusion of the original syllogism. Hence, we are forced to conclude that Toulmin's abandonment of the requirement of logical entailment between the premises and conclusion of his moral syllogism leads him to a self-contradiction. He must admit that from the same set of premises it follows equally legitimately that we have a duty to do and not to do a certain act.

There is only one way in which Toulmin can avoid this self-contradiction. That is to assume the truth of his own analytic theory from the beginning. From such a vantage point he can rule out as illegitimate all arguments that do not conform. But what will he have gained? It is quite true that everyone must grant that Toulmin's theory is correct, and that any opposed theory is mistaken, if they all begin by assuming that it is correct. But this leaves unanswered the question: *Is* the theory correct? In other words, it simply begs the question at issue. What Toulmin is, in effect, saying to the moral skeptics is: I have a theory that solves the problem of moral knowledge and vindicates moral obligation. Of course, to make it work I have to give up thinking logically. Once I have done that I find myself driven into self-contradiction, which, to avoid, all that I can do to establish my theory is to assume its truth ahead of time. Should a skeptic be impressed?

At the very beginning of this book (1.2) I introduced the term "deductive fallacy." I said then that I did not want this term to be question-begging, being willing to leave open the possibility that the so-called fallacy is not fallacious at all. Toulmin has attempted to argue a position based on the assumption that it is not a fallacy but he has failed. In fact I have demonstrated the failure of his theory. On these grounds I shall retract my original qualification to assert flatly that the deductive fallacy *is* a fallacy, and will proceed accordingly henceforth. No theory, Toulmin's included, that attempts to derive an "ought" from an "is" can succeed in answering Hume.

6. SUMMARY COMMENTS ON TOULMIN'S MORAL THEORY

Before leaving Toulmin I should like to add a few concluding remarks. These are not meant to be logical criticisms of his theory—I have given those already—but rather comments of a general nature derived from reflecting on the solution he offers to the problem of moral knowledge in relation both to those offered by other writers and to the opposed views of the moral skeptics. Toulmin, it seems to me, makes the whole business too *easy*. As one reads *The Place of Reason in Ethics* the impression grows that Toulmin does not take the problem quite seriously. Throughout, his attitude toward the arguments for moral skepticism seems to be one of blithe insouciance. On the rare occasions on which he takes notice of the skeptics, he dismisses them briefly and almost contemptuously, for example, by labelling them psychopaths (as in his reply to Bertrand Russell) or by avoiding the need to answer their objections by the debater's technique of a rhetorical counter-question (as he does in the quotation with which this chapter begins). To mention just one name at random, as far as I know Toulmin nowhere in his book refers to Nietzsche. Now Nietzsche is not a moral skeptic, yet it takes little imagination to visualize his response to a theory that holds that we have a duty to do certain acts because people in general accept such acts to be their duties. Is Nietzsche so unimportant and his views on morality so obviously unworthy of consideration that, even though they are directly opposed to Toulmin's conclusions, Toulmin does not find it necessary even so much as to refer to him? I do not believe that Nietzsche can be brushed aside so easily. Rather, it seems to me that a person advocating a view like Toulmin's ought to show how it can answer Nietzsche's arguments. This will serve as an example; there are many other writers, some skeptics and some not, whose opposition to his views Toulmin has dismissed with, at most, a passing remark. If our search is for reassuring answers and even, perhaps, for answers adequate to the practical requirements of daily life, Toulmin may very well be able to satisfy our need. But if our search is for philosophically satisfying answers, that is, answers that can stand up under strenuous and sustained critical attack, then Toulmin has little to offer.

7. NOWELL-SMITH AND THE PROBLEM OF MORAL KNOWLEDGE

Nowell-Smith's *Ethics* is a book that can be highly recommended to anyone interested in a general discussion of the field of ethics from an analytic point of view. The early chapters contain many incisive criticisms of various traditional ethical theories but the bulk of the book is devoted to an elucidation of the language used in ordinary moral discourse and, in particular, of the logical connections among the terms employed in this discourse. The book raises so many intriguing questions that the temptation to launch into a full scale critical analysis of it is hard to resist. However, such an enterprise, since it would carry us too far from the problem with which we are concerned, must be foregone. In the discussion that follows, I shall instead concentrate on just one paragraph of the book. This paragraph is of particular importance for our problem because in it Nowell-Smith states conclusions regarding moral knowledge quite different from those of Toulmin. What I shall do is to amplify these conclusions (which Nowell-Smith puts very briefly), explain why he reaches them, and draw out some of the implications that follow from them.

Before beginning it is necessary to insert an explanatory comment. Nowell-Smith's *Ethics* was originally published in 1954. In 1957 a new edition, by a different publisher, appeared. The new edition is, to the best of my knowledge, identical in its contents with the original. However, in it the author has added a short preface, in which he explains very briefly the changes that have taken place in recent years in the way in which moral philosophers—and, in particular, analysts— approach their subject, concluding with a summary statement of the results that can, and cannot be derived from such an approach. Since my concern here is with his summary statement, I shall reproduce it complete:

"Philosophical arguments, thus considered [*i.e.*, from the point of view of the analysts], have no direct bearing on moral questions. From a study of the uses of language no conclusions about what we ought to do can follow, but such a study can be helpful towards the formulation and solution of moral problems in many ways and it has an intellectual interest of its own. It can, for example, illuminate for us the complexity, versatility and precision of the language which we all, philosophers and laymen alike, use in this field, attributes which older methods tended to obscure. Nor is it necessary that the mind of a philosopher be always fixed on philosophical issues. I shall be neither surprised nor sorry if my own moral sentiments are clearly visible beneath the surface."[1]

The most notable point that emerges from this statement is the marked difference between Nowell-Smith's conclusion regarding the possibility of a philosophical solution to the problem of moral knowledge and that reached by Toulmin. Whereas Toulmin held that we can legitimately derive conclusions about what we ought to do from a study of the way in which people use moral language Nowell-Smith denies this to be possible. His brief statement, in which he rejects Toulmin's view, "From a study of the uses of language no conclusions about what we ought to do can follow," can stand some amplification. What he has in mind may be put as follows: We have two types of statement or conclusion, which must be distinguished from each other, the one linguistic and the other (to use Toulmin's term) substantial. Any conclusions (or generalizations) derived by a moral philosopher from his observation of the way in which (moral) language is actually used belong to the first type. They are linguistic conclusions (*i.e.*, generalizations about linguistic usage). On the other hand any assertions, whomever made by, to the effect that someone has a duty to do a certain act (or any similar moral judgments) belong to the second type. They are substantial assertions (*i.e.*, beliefs or convictions about substantial moral—as distinguished from linguistic—matters). Now Nowell-Smith is contending that it is impossible to present a cogent argument whose premises are entirely linguistic (descriptive of ordinary linguistic usage) in character but whose conclusion is substantial. He is denying, in effect, that the appeal to ordinary usage can provide *good reasons* for our moral convictions. Thus he directly repudiates Toulmin's claims regarding the possibility of providing a solution to the problem of moral knowledge on the analysts' assumptions. The fact of this difference of opinion between these two analysts on such a fundamental issue is interesting; more important, however, is the reason for the difference. I shall pursue this point further a bit later but, before doing so, I should like to make a few comments on the remainder of Nowell-Smith's summary statement.

In the final sentence of the quotation Nowell-Smith refers to his "moral sentiments" lurking just "beneath the surface" of the argu-

---

[1] P. H. Nowell-Smith, *Ethics* (Oxford, 1957), pp. 7–8.

ment. What does he mean by this reference and why does he make it? What he undoubtedly is referring to—and this is clear from the text of his book—is his own convictions on substantial moral issues, his personal beliefs regarding good and evil, moral obligation, and so on. What he is implying is that these moral convictions of his are expressions of personal sentiment or feeling. Thus he is placing himself within the "sentimentalist" tradition of Hume and his followers. The reason why he should do so is fairly apparent. Believing that it is impossible to provide good (*i.e.*, cogent) reasons for his moral convictions, he is forced to the conclusion that these convictions are irrational (*i.e.*, cannot be justified by argument or reason). Of course it does not follow that he must therefore believe them to be expressions of sentiment, yet this alternative has proved attractive to many moral philosophers forced to similar skeptical conclusions. It is thus not unexpected that Nowell-Smith should accept it as well.

Having, at the beginning of his statement, denied the (analyst) moral philosopher the ability to provide any arguments in support of substantial moral conclusions, Nowell-Smith then proceeds to indicate some alternative tasks that he can perform. Two are distinguished. The moral philosopher can help in "the formulation and solution of moral problems in many ways" and he can "illuminate for us the complexity, versatility and precision of the language which we all... use in this field." Both of these assertions about the tasks and competencies of the moral philosopher, it seems to me, raise questions. In the first place, I wonder if Nowell-Smith's belief that the moral philosopher can help solve moral problems is consistent with his denial that any conclusions about what we ought to do can follow from a study of the uses of language. Just what moral problems can the philosopher help to solve? It might be objected here that it is unfair to ask such a question of Nowell-Smith, in this context. For the statement from which I am quoting is only a very brief summary so he can hardly be expected to elaborate such a point in it; to find his answer to my question one must read his whole book. However, such an objection misses the point. For the problem I am concerned with is not a consequence of the brevity of Nowell-Smith's statement but of an apparent logical incompatibility between assertions he makes within it. When he speaks of the "moral problems" the philosopher can help to solve, he appears to be referring to substantial (rather than linguistic) matters, to the kind of problems embodied in questions such as "What act ought I to do in this situation?" and "Why ought I to do it?" But it is just such questions, he has already admitted, with which the moral philosopher, in his exclusive concern with our uses of language, is powerless to deal.

The other job that Nowell-Smith gives to the moral philosopher, to illuminate the complexity, versatility, and precision of our moral language, is certainly one that he can perform. No better evidence for this is needed than that given by the brilliant work done by Nowell-Smith himself in *Ethics*. Yet a problem remains. For Nowell-Smith goes on to point out that the performance of this task is an element in the work of the moral philosopher that "older methods often tended to obscure." The truth of this contention may be challenged but I think that to do so would be to miss the real point. Rather, one should reply to Nowell-Smith that, insofar as older methods of moral philosophy or, to speak more directly, traditional moral philosophers, paid scant attention to our ordinary moral language, they did so because they did not conceive it to be the aim of moral philosophy to "illuminate" this language. As philosophers their purpose instead was to solve theoretical problems, to provide answers to questions like "What kinds of acts ought we to do?" and, more particularly, to find reasons for the answers they gave to such questions. The reason why traditional philosophers have not devoted the kind of attention to our ordinary moral language that Nowell-Smith does is that they have believed their concern as moral philosophers to be with substantial, rather than with linguistic problems.

There are two grounds on which Nowell-Smith can criticize traditional philosophers for their failure to devote sufficient attention to a study of ordinary moral language. He might argue, first, that this failure has impeded them in their attempts to cope with the substantial issues with which they are concerned. However, this line of attack is cut off to him because he has already admitted that linguistic studies cannot provide answers to substantial questions. Or he might argue (as he undoubtedly would) that moral philosophy is incompetent to deal with substantial issues at all, hence that traditional moral philosophers have been misguided in their efforts. They ought to give up trying to find good reasons for our moral convictions and devote their attention to some other task, specifically, to the illumination of our moral language. This criticism would be just *if* Nowell-Smith were able to show that the attempt to deal philosophically with substantial moral issues, in the way that traditional philosophers have tried to do, really is futile. This, however, he has by no means done. Granted that he has (in his book) raised serious objections to many traditional theories and granted, further, that he has shown that we cannot, with the tools of the analysts, ever cope with substantial moral issues, he has not shown the enterprise of moral philosophy (as traditionally conceived) to be hopeless. Many philosophers would, despite the criticisms of Nowell-Smith and others, defend the possibility of coping with such issues by traditional means. And even if all such approaches to these problems should finally fail, there may be a solution that we do not have the ability to articulate or even yet to grasp. At least this, I think, can be said—as long as the skeptics have not demonstrated to us the futility of our enterprise, philosophers should still be granted the opportunity to carry on with it. And should the skeptics ever succeed in demonstrating to us the impossibility of accomplishing our aim, that will be time enough to turn our attention from substantial moral issues to the illumination of moral language. Perhaps, however, it will be past time; under such conditions it might be better that we simply give up the pretence of moral philosophy.

So much for my general comments on Nowell-Smith's statement. I should like to return now to the point with which I began the discussion—his disagreement with Toulmin on the question of whether it is possible to derive substantial moral conclusions from arguments whose premises are linguistic in nature. I then raised, but did not answer the question: Why does Nowell-Smith reach the negative conclusion that he does? Actually the answer is quite simple. As he makes clear subsequently, he does so because he believes any argument that attempts to reach a conclusion that contains an "ought" from a set of premises that do not—and this would include all arguments from linguistic premises to substantial moral conclusions—is guilty of what I have termed the deductive fallacy.[1] So we find ourselves with two analytic moral philosophers, one believing that a description of the moral language that people ordinarily use can provide a justification for conclusions about what we ought to do, hence can provide a basis for moral knowledge, while the other maintains that this cannot be done. And the reason for their opposition is their disagreement over the deductive fallacy.

From what I have said in § 5 it is fairly obvious that I agree with Nowell-Smith against Toulmin on this point. I believe that his statement "from a study of the uses of language no conclusion about what we ought to do can follow" is true. However, I have some doubts about the propriety of Nowell-Smith's making it. As an analyst Nowell-

---

[1] Cf. *ibid.*, pp. 32–33, 200, and 225.

Smith presumably accepts the Wittgensteinian thesis that the task of the philosopher is simply the description of ordinary usage. In fact his very assertion of the conclusion I have just quoted (taken along with the rest of what he says in his summary statement) implies his acceptance of that thesis in the realm of moral philosophy. But this assertion implies, as I have already argued, something more; namely, his acceptance of the assumption that for a conclusion to follow legitimately from a set of premises it must be logically deducible from them. It is because he accepts this assumption that he holds that any theory, like Toulmin's, which attempts to derive substantial moral conclusions from a study of the uses of language is untenable. Now my question is this: Is Nowell-Smith's acceptance of the Wittgensteinian thesis about the task of the philosopher compatible with the view implied in his assertion about the nature of logical deduction? If we interpret his assertion in terms of his own general analytic position, what he must be understood to mean when he says "from a study of the uses of language no conclusions about what we ought to do can follow" is something like the following: "From my observations of the way in which people ordinarily use the terms in question I find that they do not say that they draw conclusions about what they ought to do, and that these are logically deducible from a study of the uses of language." But such an interpretation of the assertion clearly travesties Nowell-Smith's intent. What he obviously means by the assertion is that conclusions about what we ought to do *cannot* follow, in the traditional logical deductive sense, from descriptive premises about language uses. We must, thus, conclude that, in reaching this conclusion, Nowell-Smith has momentarily abandoned his analytic theory and lapsed into a traditional philosophical position. This he could perhaps justify, defending himself by saying that he accepts the Wittgensteinian position in the area of moral philosophy but not in logic. The situation would have been clarified, however, if he had been more explicit on this point, and also if he had explained his reasons for not making his adoption of Wittgensteinian analysis a thoroughgoing one. What reasons, if any, could Nowell-Smith give for believing that the analytic point of view, although not viable in logic, is so in moral philosophy?

But what would happen if, for an experiment, we were to interpret Nowell-Smith's assertion in the manner I have suggested, *i.e.*, consistently with an analytic theory of the nature of logical relationships? Could we on that basis reach the same negative answer that he reaches? Could we, that is, legitimately come to the conclusion that it is impossible to derive any conclusion about what we ought to do from a study of the uses of language? No, we could not. For any attempt to do so would fall victim to the same kinds of objections that I urged (in § 5) against Toulmin's analytic argument for the opposite conclusion.

Still a question remains, not about Nowell-Smith but about analysis in general. What I have been doing throughout this chapter is examining the claim made by analytic moral philosophy, as exemplified particularly by Toulmin, to solve the problem of moral knowledge and thus to offer an acceptable alternative to moral skepticism. According to Toulmin, it is possible, if we adopt the analytic point of view, to provide good (*i.e.*, cogent) reasons for our convictions about what we ought to do. We have found, however, that Toulmin could not sustain this claim. The reasonable skeptic will not, and need not, be disturbed in his views by the arguments advanced by Toulmin. Going further, we have found that, if one adopts the analytic point of view in general, applying it in logic as well as in ethics, he is unable to maintain that conclusions about what we ought to do either *do* or *do not* follow from premises about the uses of language. From a study of the uses of language, the only conclusions that anyone can legitimately reach will be statements about the uses of language—and nothing else. The analyst thus can provide no help to those trying to find an alternative to moral skepticism. In addition, he is equally unable to give any comfort to the skeptic. For the writings of the analysts are *systematically irrelevant* to the problem of moral knowledge.

8. WITTGENSTEIN AND THE REVOLUTION IN PHILOSOPHY

In this chapter I have tried to give specific arguments showing why the analysts' attempts to solve the problem of moral knowledge fail. In doing so I have kept the discussion generally within the realm of moral philosophy itself. Such a procedure runs the risk of being misleading, by conveying the impression that the analysts' failure stems from shortcomings within their *moral* theory. I should like, in this section, very briefly to counteract any such impression, which is a definite misconception. For the shortcomings of the analysts' moral philosophy, rather than being basic, are simply one expression of a fundamental error, lying in the original assumptions of analysis in general. The onus for the failure of analytic moral philosophy thus lies not with Toulmin or Nowell-Smith but with Wittgenstein. For Wittgensteinian analysis is an untenable philosophical position.

Wittgenstein truly launched a revolution in philosophy. The revolutionary character of his thought is unquestionably his most significant contribution to twentieth-century philosophy. But it is also the fatal flaw in the philosophy of analysis that he created. For Wittgenstein's philosophical revolution is self-defeating.

According to Wittgenstein traditional philosophers have been guilty, almost universally, of a fundamental error. They have conceived it to be their task to *explain* the world. But this the philosopher cannot do. Instead of trying to explain, he must instead simply describe. And what he is to describe is ordinary language, as he observes it being used. In Wittgenstein's words, "Philosophy may in no way interfere with the actual use of language; it can in the end only describe it." To use symmetrical terms, one could call the difference between Wittgensteinian analysis and traditional philosophy a difference between philosophy conceived of as *descriptive* and as *prescriptive*. Traditional philosophical theories are prescriptive. As theoretical explanations of reality, they set up norms which our ordinary discourse must satisfy if it is to qualify as veridical. For example, materialism holds the universe to be composed solely of matter in motion. Hence spiritual beings cannot exist. On the basis of his theory, the materialist prescribes the kind of language we can, and cannot legitimately use, Hobbes, for instance, pointing out that the locution "immaterial substance" is self-contradictory. And so with other traditional theories. Because they purport to provide true explanations of reality, they consider themselves qualified to sit in judgment on the way we talk, prescribing what is legitimate and what is not. By denying the philosopher the ability to explain reality, Wittgenstein takes from him his prescriptive power. Rather than being qualified to sit in judgment on our ordinary language, the philosopher must content himself simply with describing it.

The crucial question that Wittgenstein must face is this: Can philosophy completely avoid prescriptions and become purely descriptive? For this to be possible no philosophical theory could ever lay down a prescription or set up a norm. But how can any philosophical theory—and, specifically, Wittgenstein's—maintain that philosophy *must* be simply descriptive *without* in that very act itself becoming prescriptive? The thesis that the sole legitimate function of philosophers is to describe ordinary usage, which is the heart of the Wittgensteinian revolution, is not itself descriptive but on the contrary prescriptive. In the very act of enunciating his theory Wittgenstein is forced logically to violate the prescription he lays down in it. When applied to itself his theory proves self-contradictory. Hence he is logically prevented from ever even stating it.

There is one way in which my objection may be countered—by the reply that Wittgenstein's thesis is not prescriptive at all but really descriptive, hence is not self-contradictory. Logically, such a reply is impeccable. Yet will it do? If his thesis is descriptive, then his statement "Philosophy may in no way interfere with the actual use of language; it can in the end only describe it" must be interpreted, not as laying down a prescription as it appears to be doing, but to mean something like the following, "As the word 'philosophy' is ordinarily used, it refers to an activity whose practitioners are engaged in the description of language uses but who never interfere with those uses which they are describing." It is hardly necessary to point out that such a generalization, even if it could be taken seriously, is flagrantly false. But this is not the real objection to a "descriptive" rendition of Wittgenstein's thesis. Rather it is the following: If the thesis is interpreted as a descriptive generalization about the ordinary use of a word, it can not operate as a ban on the activity of philosophizing, in the traditional sense. Philosophers—or, if this title is denied them, "metaphysicians," "thinkers," "speculators," or whatever new name such people care to assume—can continue their traditional activities of theory formation and can sit in judgment on our ordinary uses of language with impunity, as far as Wittgenstein is concerned. For he has done nothing which can deny them these activities; all he has done is to tell us (erroneously) how the word "philosophy" is ordinarily used. And such information is totally irrelevant to the question of whether or not men can legitimately speculate and theorize about the nature of reality.

But the objection might be raised, What follows from all this? Granted that a "descriptive" interpretation of Wittgenstein's thesis makes that thesis irrelevant to the question of the legitimacy of speculative inquiry, why does this constitute a criticism of such an interpretation? The answer is: It completely undermines Wittgenstein's *revolution* in philosophy. Why is Wittgenstein one of the most important and influential thinkers of the twentieth century? Because he proclaimed the "revolutionary" thesis that he had discovered that the word "philosophy" is ordinarily applied to the activity of describing language uses? The point does not really require arguing. What makes Wittgenstein significant is that he did inaugurate a revolution. He believed that he had found a way of eliminating traditional philosophy by showing that the entire enterprise is illegitimate. His thesis was to provide a criterion in terms of which philosophical activity could be judged, the traditional method of theoretical explanation eliminated as illegitimate, and the rationale stated for an entirely new conception of philosophy, the revolutionary notion of philosophy as the description of ordinary language. But for these significant goals to be achieved, the thesis enunciated by Wittgenstein *must* be considered to be prescriptive, hence must be rejected as self-contradictory. Wittgenstein's revolution in philosophy has not been realized. The reason, however, is not that he did not attempt to accomplish a revolution but that the revolution for which he hoped is logically impossible of achievement.

What, it might be asked, led Wittgenstein to believe he could, or should revolutionize philosophy? Any answer to such a question must be partly guesswork; however I am inclined to think that after the first war he came to the conclusion that the theory underlying his *Tractatus* was untenable. He became convinced, whether rightly or not is immaterial, that the line of philosophizing represented by that work was a dead end. Having rejected his own earlier beliefs he decided, for what could not but be inadequate reasons, that all traditional philosophy suffered from the same fatal defects as his own theories. The ordinary language analysis of the later Wittgenstein may thus be viewed as his own repudiation of his earlier self, generalized to include a repudiation of earlier philosophical thought as a whole. Yet in his own case the break with the past is far from complete. For there is a prophetic irony in the concluding sentence of the *Tractatus*.

CHAPTER VI

A RETURN TO INTUITIONISM

How significant for the problem of moral knowledge is the conclusion we reached in the last chapter? I think it would be less than realistic to assume that we have simply found another attempted solution to the problem to have failed. The situation is more serious than that. For the analysts, in spite of the weakness of their Wittgensteinian assumptions, have been acutely aware of the problem posed by Hume's critique of moral arguments and have set out deliberately to seek a justification for our moral beliefs that would not fall prey to the deductive fallacy. Their failure, thus, does more than destroy their own theory; it strongly reinforces the conclusion that no theory of moral knowledge can be successful. Although we might, despite the discouraging results of the last four chapters, still continue the search for an acceptable theory (*i.e.*, argument that would provide a rational justification for our beliefs about what we ought to do), I think it is safe to predict before we begin that, in some way or other, any such theory would come to grief over the deductive fallacy. It would either commit a *non-sequitur* or lead into an infinite regress. Should we then abandon the search and bow to moral skepticism? Before making this move, I should like to try once more to find a rational basis for our moral convictions.

1. THE DEDUCTIVE FALLACY, SKEPTICISM, AND INTUITIONISM

If we grant, as I think we must, that any attempt to provide a justification for our beliefs about what we ought to do by means of an *argument* inevitably commits the deductive fallacy, we must look for an answer to skepticism in a view that justifies these beliefs without recourse to any argument. Now we have found only one such position in the course of our discussion, namely, intuitionism. I have examined two different forms of intuitionistic theory of moral obligation in the book, (1) intuitionistic utilitarianism, which holds that the proposition "It is always our duty to do the act which in the circumstances will produce the best consequences possible" is intuitively self-evident (see Chapter II, esp. 2.7), and (2) the deontological view of Prichard and Ross, which holds it to be self-evident that certain acts like promise-keeping, truth-telling, and so on are *prima facie* duties (see Chapter III). In this chapter I should like to turn once again to intuitionism to see if some way can be discovered by which it can be defended against the attacks of the skeptics and a theoretical justification of moral knowledge founded on it. Since I shall be concerned here with intuitionism in general, I shall not distinguish between the different forms it has taken but shall concentrate on the deontology of Prichard and Ross, using it as an example of intuitionism. The conclusions that I reach regarding deontology can easily be applied to any other form of intuitionistic account of moral knowledge. Before I return to intuitionism, however, I should face some obvious initial objections to my proposal.

It might be said that to return at this stage of the argument to intuitionism would be a waste of time. I admit that the chances of success do not appear very good but the situation is desperate so desperate measures are called for. This point, at least, intuitionism has in its favor: it is the only theory we have found that successfully avoids the deductive fallacy. But then, it might be asked, what was the purpose of Chapter III? Was intuitionism not successfully disposed of there? My reply to this query must be ambiguous. I think that in Chapter III I made good my case that Prichard and Ross have not succeeded in producing a single assertion about what we ought to do that a reasonable skeptic need admit to be true. In this respect they have failed. On the other hand, I did not demonstrate the impossibility of there being such an assertion. Furthermore, as some readers may have noted, my criticisms of the deontologists in Chapter III (excluding §'s 5 and 6) were themselves based on an appeal to direct moral intuition. I contended (particularly in § 4) that I myself (and most other people as well) do not directly apprehend a moral obligation to act in certain situations in the way we should do, if the deontologists' views about our duties were true. On the contrary, our moral intuitions are quite at variance with what the deontologists say they should be. My criticisms of the deontologists, because based on an appeal to intuition themselves, are thus not logically conclusive. More than that, they destroy not intuitionism itself but at best simply the specific intuitions of the deontologists. So the question might be raised: *Can* intuitionism be demolished? If not, there may be some hope that it can be rehabilitated in such a way that it can provide a viable alternative to moral skepticism. To resolve this issue we must see if we can discover logical arguments, in contradistinction to intuitive appeals, capable either of lending support to intuitionism or of ruling it decisively out of consideration as a theory of moral knowledge. In this chapter my object will be to find such logical arguments.

2. A DEFENSE OF INTUITIONISM

I shall begin the argument with a general defense of intuitionism. To accomplish this perhaps the best way to start is to ask how intuitionism might be attacked. Since the issue will turn on logical considerations, rather than going through a long list of specific lines of attack, I shall examine two general modes of criticism, which between them are exhaustive. Intuitionism may be attacked either from the inside or from the outside. The critic, that is to say, may either accept or deny the possibility that intuition can yield us knowledge of what we ought to do. If he takes the first alternative, he will then have to go on to argue that, although intuitive moral knowledge is a possibility, it is not an actuality.

Let us begin with the external critic, who denies the possibility of intuitive moral knowledge. He can attack intuitionism from several points of view, each increasingly liberal. He might argue from a completely skeptical position, denying the possibility of knowledge at all, hence of moral knowledge, hence of intuition as a basis for moral knowledge. Or he might accept the possibility of certain kinds of knowledge but deny that of moral knowledge. Or, finally, he might admit the possibility of moral knowledge but deny that it can be gained by means of intuition.

The absolute skeptic can be disposed of quickly. His thesis is self-contradictory so logically untenable. The arguments of the other two types of external critic, however, are much less easy to dispose of so will require considerable examination before they can be evaluated. Those who take either of the two remaining positions agree with each other (against the absolute skeptic) in believing knowledge to be possible but differ in their views as to what can be known, one group admitting and the other denying that moral obligations are legitimate items of knowledge. They appear to differ from each other in a second respect also, the moral skeptic rejecting intuitive moral knowledge not because it rests on intuition but because it asserts the reality of moral knowledge and the moral believer, on the other hand, rejecting it, not because it asserts the reality of moral knowledge, but because it rests this assertion on an appeal to intuition. In actuality, however, this distinction very probably misrepresents the facts of the situation, for most moral skeptics would directly reject intuitionism as a method for gaining moral knowledge. Their moral skepticism results from their further contention that no other method can be any more successful than intuition in yielding such knowledge. So we can conclude with some confidence that among the chief reasons why both types of critic reject the possibility of intuitive moral knowledge is that it is intuitive. The main thrust of their attack against moral intuitionism is directed not against what is known but rather against the way in which it is alleged to be known.

If this analysis is fair, then both types of critic appear to be guilty of the genetic fallacy. They are arguing that an alleged item of knowledge cannot be a real item of knowledge because of the way in which the knower came by it. But does conviction of the genetic fallacy in this case dispose of these critics? For might they not argue in reply that here the "genetic fallacy" is not a fallacy at all? We must, at least, look further into the situation. Let us suppose that each of two people says "X is Y and I know that this is true." But each person has reached this conclusion by a different procedure—observation, deduction, intuition, revelation, or whatever. Now person A contends that, although he knows that X is Y, person B does not because the procedure he has used in reaching the conclusion is unacceptable. Can A defend his contention? Assuming that X is Y, we can say that A and B both believe with equal conviction the true proposition "X is Y." For A to contend that he has knowledge and B has not thus appears to be self-contradictory because he is implying by this that the belief that X is Y is both knowledge and not knowledge. A, however, might counter this objection by arguing that it rests on the assumption, which he rejects, that true belief is a sufficient criterion of knowledge. On the contrary, he might contend, a person may firmly believe something that is true yet not know it. Such a situation, he might then go on to add, obtains whenever the true belief concerns an assertion of duty and the grounds for the belief are moral intuition.

I think that most people would agree with A's position that true belief is not a sufficient criterion for knowledge. Unless we did so, we should be forced to make some further distinction, between "knowledge" and "well-grounded" or "justified" knowledge. Without such a distinction there would be no difference, as far as its knowledge-status is concerned, between my belief, based on a sheer guess, that there are X number of beans in a bowl, when as a matter of fact there are exactly that number there, and my same belief, gained by having carefully counted the beans as they were dropped in. The point in A's case that is open to question is not his contention that a true belief may sometimes not constitute knowledge but his further thesis that no moral belief based on intuition can qualify as knowledge. To defend this thesis, he would have to establish that no moral conclusion gained through intuition can satisfy the criteria that a proposition must fulfil in order to qualify as an item of knowledge. To do this he would have to set up knowledge criteria that would exclude beliefs based on moral intuition. But what kind of knowledge criteria could these be? He could not include among them the criterion that knowledge must be gained by means other than intuition because, if he did, he would beg the question at issue. In effect he would be arguing that intuition cannot yield moral knowledge for the reason that intuition cannot yield moral knowledge. In order to rule out intuitionism, he would have to set up knowledge criteria which in some other, indirect way made it impossible for any proposition whose truth was defended by an appeal to intuition to qualify as an item of knowledge.

Let us assume for purposes of argument that A could articulate some such set of criteria. Could he use these to rule intuitive propositions out of court? If he tried to do so, how would he defend himself against an intuitionist who, after admitting that, if the criteria are accepted, intuitive moral knowledge is impossible, then went on to deny that the criteria themselves are definitive for knowledge? Faced with such a challenge A would have to provide some defense for his knowledge criteria since failure to do so would be an admission that they are arbitrary hence incapable of ruling out intuitive propositions. He would thus be forced to give reasons for holding these criteria to be definitive for knowledge.

To put the point in slightly different terms, in order to qualify his criteria as criteria for knowledge A would have to establish that they are the true criteria and that he knows them to be so. But the final requirement is one that he could not fulfil. To establish that he knows that the criteria in question are the true criteria for knowledge he would have to appeal to some knowledge criterion or set of criteria. What might these criteria be? Logically, there are only two possibilities. The criteria would have to be either (1) the same as or (2) different from the knowledge criteria that he has used in rejecting intuitionism and that the intuitionist has now demanded that he justify. If they were the same as the original criteria they could not possibly justify these criteria because the whole justification procedure would then be question-begging. If the criteria appealed to were different from those that they were being used to justify, the assertion that the original criteria were really knowledge criteria (which the whole process of justification was meant to establish) would have to be given up. However, there is an even more serious problem here. For whatever the criteria appealed to at this stage of the argument, the intuitionist might challenge them in turn, forcing his critic once again to justify them by an appeal to some further set of criteria. Thus the entire procedure would have to be repeated. And so on *ad infinitum*.

To sum up, it is impossible from a standpoint outside of intuitionism to destroy the intuitionists' view that moral knowledge may be gained by direct insight. For anyone who contends that knowledge of what we ought to do cannot be gained by moral intuition, if he is asked to justify himself, can be forced to admit either that his stand is arbitrary, or that it begs the question, or that any attempt to support it leads him into an infinite regress.

But if intuitionism cannot be destroyed from the outside, can it be demolished from the inside? Can one admit the possibility of intuitive moral knowledge and yet deny its actuality? As far as our problem is concerned this is probably an academic question; for no moral skeptic, I am sure, would be willing to admit the possibility and simply deny the actuality of intuitive moral truths. For him there are none because there can be none. However, let us see what might be said on the issue. We must begin with the fact that intuitionists believe that there are many moral propositions whose truth they intuit to be self-evident. What the critic must show is that, although such propositions *might* be directly intuited to be true, in fact they are not. Nor can he simply assert his view; to do that would be quite arbitrary and unwarranted. He must give some reasons for what he says. Probably the most obvious line for him to take would be the one I used against the deontologists' view that it is self-evident that we always have a (*prima facie*) duty to keep our promises, when I cited the case (in 3.4) of a promise made to the kidnapper of one's child and then argued that I fail to intuit any duty of promise-keeping in such a situation. If one could sustain the same kind of objection against all moral truths alleged to be self-evident by intuitionists, he might then say that he finds none of these to qualify as an item of knowledge.

There are serious objections to such a position, taken as a method of refuting moral intuitionism. In the first place it is not conclusive. Although I believe that the conclusion I reached in the kidnapping case in 3.4 is correct and therefore that Prichard and Ross are mistaken in believing that they intuit a duty to keep promises as such, I cannot demonstrate this point. They can still claim that they *do* intuit such a duty. And there is just the possibility that they are right. But a more important point is involved here. This concerns the considerations which led me to my conclusion. For I did not simply fail to intuit any obligation to keep a promise in this situation. What prompted me to deny the obligation was my reflection on the case, which led me to the conclusion that the promise given would not be binding. In other words, my conclusion, as much as that of the deontologists, rested on intuition. Although I disagreed with their intuition, my disagreement assumed not only that we can, by intuition, discover moral truths but that I had in fact done so. The truth I believed that I had directly intuited is that we are morally justified in breaking a promise made to a kidnapper. Although this truth does not assert a moral obligation—in fact, it presupposes one—it does, if it is really true, give us an item of moral knowledge of a type that no moral skeptic could ever admit.

But need a critic follow the line I took? Might he not say that he fails to intuit any of the obligations claimed to be self-evident by the intuitionists, not because these conflict with other moral insights he has, but simply because, when he regards the situation in question, no intuition comes? Certainly he might do so. But, if he did, what reason would we have for agreeing with him? If he is right, then the intuitionists are all hallucinating; if they are right, he suffers from moral blindness. And on what rational basis can we choose between the two? At this point we must give up argument and resort to name-calling. For if we agree that the intuitionists have no way of demonstrating their position against such a critic, we must equally admit that he has no way of demonstrating his against them. But in the present argument the burden of proof rests with the critic of intuitionism; he has to show that none of their intuitive insights constitutes an item of knowledge.

In summary, I think that a good case can be made for the thesis that intuitionism is invulnerable to attack. As long as a person contends that he is completely clear about what he is doing, is not confused or misled, and then asserts that he is having a crystal-clear intuition of a duty to perform a certain act or kind of act—and the deontologists, for example, do all of these—there is no way that he can be demonstrated to be mistaken. A critic may be convinced, for any number of reasons, that the person is mistaken but he has no way conclusively of showing this to be true. And to be convinced that your opponent is mistaken and to be able to present an argument capable of demonstrating that he is are two quite different things. If this is so then the attacks on intuitionism may not be so effective as they might have seemed. In fact, we may have been premature in writing intuition off as a possible way of answering the skeptics. Perhaps there is much more to be said for it than we have been willing to grant.

Before we get our hopes raised about the possibility of rehabilitating intuitionism as a theory of moral knowledge, however, we must note one important point about the conclusions we have just reached: they are all negative. To concede that intuitionism may be invulnerable to attack is to admit only that the moral assertions of the intuitionists cannot be demonstrated to be false. It is not to imply that they are true. Nor, even more important, is it to admit that the intuitionists have given any good reasons for believing them to be true. But if intuitionism is to establish itself as an acceptable theory of moral knowledge it must do these things. It must move from the defensive to the offensive. So the burden of the argument shifts from the critic of intuitionism to the intuitionist himself. What can he say in support of his position? Can he give any good reasons for believing that his moral intuitions are true? If so what are they? To answer these questions successfully, the intuitionists must overcome two serious obstacles. I shall consider them in turn.

3. KNOWLEDGE AND A PLURALITY OF INTUITIONS

In Chapter I (1.4) I set up two general conditions of knowledge. If a proposition is to qualify as an item of knowledge, (1) what it asserts must be true and (2) one must be able to provide good reasons for holding that what it asserts is true. The first is a necessary but not a sufficient condition of knowledge; but the second is both necessary and sufficient. If intuitionism is to justify itself as a satisfactory theory of moral knowledge the intuitionists must be able to show that the propositions they assert to be self-evidently true and hence items of knowledge succeed in satisfying these two conditions of knowledge.

Let us begin with the first condition, asking whether any of the propositions that the intuitionists claim to be items of knowledge actually are true. Immediately, however, we are faced with problems.

For how are we going to determine whether any of these propositions are true? To what criterion of truth shall we appeal in reaching our judgment? And even if we were to discover that no proposition alleged by the intuitionists to be an item of knowledge is in fact true, how could we use this evidence for any general conclusion that intuitionism is not a satisfactory theory of moral knowledge? For another intuition, which we had not considered and which would prove on examination to be true, might well be forth-coming. Rather than attempting to answer these questions, I should like to take a different tack, by raising the following question: Can any of the propositions that intuitionists have actually claimed to be self-evidently true be demonstrated to be *false*? If this can be done, then these propositions, which they have asserted to be items of knowledge, *cannot* be items of knowledge. We shall thus have shown that acceptance of intuitive self-evidence as a criterion of knowledge has led to error.

In Chapter III (3.4) I criticized the claim made by Prichard and Ross that it is self-evidently true that we have a (*prima facie*) duty to keep any promise we have made. My criticism, like their assertion, rested on an appeal to moral intuition. I argued that it was self-evidently true that sometimes we have no *prima facie* duty to keep a promise we have made. Now these two assertions-that we do and that we do not have a *prima facie* duty to keep promises as such—contradict each other. Therefore we know that one of them is true and the other one false. Or, to take another example, certain intuitionistic utilitarians have held that it is self-evidently true that we have only one duty— always to act in a way that will maximize good consequences. The deontologists hold, on the contrary, that it is self-evidently true that the duty to maximize good consequences is only one of our obligations and that, therefore, we may be obligated to do an act even though performance of that act will produce consequences less good than we could have produced by doing some other act instead. Once again, the assertions, both resting on an appeal to intuition, contradict each other. Therefore we know that one of them is true and the other one false.

The first conclusion we can draw from these examples is that certain propositions that intuitionists—whether they be deontologists, intuitionistic utilitarians, or myself in Chapter III—have asserted to be items of knowledge are not so. Because they are false, these propositions fail to satisfy the first, and necessary, condition of knowledge. This conclusion strikes a heavy blow at intuitionism. For it forces any intuitionist, on pain of self-contradiction, to admit that either he, or some other intuitionist, has held a demonstrably false proposition to be intuitively self-evident. Under these circumstances what claim can the appeal to intuition, as a basis for moral *knowledge*, have on our allegiance? A theory of moral knowledge which, on its own showing, has led philosophers to embrace error for truth, can hardly present itself as a viable alternative to moral skepticism.

But our conclusion has an observe side to it too, which an intuitionist would probably be quick to point out. Although it is logically necessary that some alleged self-evident truths of the intuitionists be false, it is equally logically necessary that some be true. Now, we must remember that moral skepticism can be avoided if we can produce a single moral proposition that we know to be true. But have not the intuitionists done just that? In fact, they can produce many. At first glance this argument may appear to be sound but I believe it to be sophistical. For consider what would happen if we were to push it to an extreme. We could in the simplest manner in the world refute the skeptics. All that we would have to do would be to assert a series of pairs of moral propositions—without appealing to intuition or anything else to justify any of them—of such a nature that one member of each pair contradicted the other. We could then conclude, on logical grounds alone, that one member of each pair is necessarily true (the other being necessarily false). However—and this is the key to the fallacy in the argument—we should never know in the case of any of the pairs, which of its two members is the true and which the false one. Thus, although we might claim that there are true moral propositions, we could never point to any such proposition and substantiate our claim that we know it to be true (for it might for all we know be the false member of the pair). It is here that our second condition of knowledge becomes operative. Before admitting a proposition to be an item of knowledge, it demands that we be able to provide good reasons for holding that proposition to be true. And these cannot be provided for us by the logical argument just given, for the same reason it gives for holding any particular moral proposition to be true it provides equally for holding that proposition to be false and its denial true.

Although the argument I have presented in this section does, I think, remove intuitionism from consideration as an answer to moral skepticism, still it is limited in a very important way. For it depends for its cogency on the fact that the intuitionists have actually claimed intuitive self-evidence for logically conflicting propositions. But what if this were not true? What if all the moral propositions that intuitionists had alleged to be self-evidently true should prove to be consistent with each other? Then we could not use this argument against intuitionism. I believe, however, that there is another argument that can be raised against the intuitionists that is not subject to this limitation but that holds good against their position no matter what the actual nature of their alleged intuitive moral truths might be. I shall turn to it now.

4. INTUITIVE SELF-EVIDENCE AND MORAL KNOWLEDGE

Intuitionists assert that they know certain moral propositions to be true. Let us assume, for purposes of argument, that we could not demonstrate that at least some of the propositions in question must be false and ask whether we have to agree with the intuitionists that they are all true and that the intuitionists can give us good reasons for believing them to be so or, for that matter, that any one of them is true and that they can give us good reasons for believing it to be so? Before the intuitionists can legitimately demand that we accept such propositions as items of knowledge, they must satisfy us on both of these points. The burden of the argument here rests with them. We are *willing* to be convinced but we must be *convinced*. The intuitionists are making a knowledge claim on behalf of certain propositions and we are simply requesting that, if they are to expect us to accept that claim, they must provide us with reasons which warrant our doing so. And if these reasons are not forthcoming, we are justified in dismissing the propositions in question as merely unsubstantiated hence unwarranted beliefs.

Can an intuitionist give us any good reasons for believing that what he intuits to be true is in fact true rather than false? He might be tempted to answer that it must be true because, if it were not, he could not intuit it to be so. But what could he mean here by the words "must" and "could not"? Do they express logical relationships? If so, a proposition of the form "A intuits X to be true and X is false" would be self-contradictory, and the proposition "Whatever A intuits to be true is true" lapses into a tautology, to the effect either that "Whatever is true is true" or "Whatever A intuits to be true he intuits to be true." But neither of these tautologies can give us any reason for believing that what A intuits to be true really is true.

The intuitionists themselves would agree with this conclusion—as they must, if they are to have a theory of moral knowledge—holding that the proposition "Whatever one intuits to be true is true" is synthetic rather than analytic. For it joins together the two different concepts of propositions which, on the one hand, are asserted, on the basis of a distinctive act of mind, to be true and, on the other, are actually true. Intuitionists would then justify the synthesis by arguing that intuition is a cognitive act of the mind by which we grasp that there is a necessary, but synthetic, connection between the subject and the predicate of certain propositions, for example, between the fact that a certain act is an act of promise-keeping and the quite different fact that the act is our duty. It is our grasp of this necessary connection between subject and predicate that warrants us in asserting as true the proposition "We have a (*prima facie*) duty to keep our promises." Because intuition enables us to grasp such necessary connections between subjects and predicates, we are justified in making the general assertion that whatever one intuits to be true is true. As Ross puts it:

"And the ultimate propositions at which we arrive seem not to express mere brute facts, but facts which are self-evidently necessary. For instance, the very object of a promise being to encourage some one to believe that one will act in a certain way, it is self-evident that he has a moral claim to our behaving in that way if he wants us to to do so.

If we now turn to ask how we come to know these fundamental moral principles, the answer seems to be that it is in the same way in which we come to know the axioms of mathematics. Both alike seem to be both synthetic and *a priori*; that is to say, we see the predicate, though not included in the definition of the subject, to belong to anything which satisfies that definition."[1]

According to Ross we grasp the necessary connection between subject and predicate of our fundamental moral principles through an act of intuition. Granted our ability to recognize moral truths directly, then whatever we so recognize must be true. Here, however, we have to be very careful. When an intuitionist says that a moral proposition he intuits to be true *must* be true, he is not using "must" in a logical sense. Logically, the proposition may be false for one who denies it would not be contradicting himself. To sum up, we know on logical grounds that some alleged intuitions may be false and we know in fact that some have proved to be false. To sustain his thesis that we can know, through an act of intuition, that certain moral proposition are

---

[1] Ross, *Foundations of Ethics*, p. 320. In the last sentence of the quotation Ross is using the word "see" as a synonym for "intuit."

true, the intuitionist must be able to distinguish between veridical and false moral intuitions. Since we must assume that the experience one has when he believes himself to be intuiting a moral truth is the same whether the intuition be veridical or false, we can put the intuitionist's problem in an extreme form by raising the questions: If some intuitions may be false, may not all be so? And how does the intuitionist know that this does not represent the actual state of affairs? How can he be sure that he is not systematically deluded in his moral intuitions? Since intuition can lead one astray, the intuitionist, in order to defend his appeal to intuition as a source of moral knowledge, must provide some criterion in terms of which he can distinguish false from veridical intuitions as well as justify his assumption that the intuitions he holds to be veridical really are so. How would he do this? Ross gives the following answer:

> "To me it seems as self-evident as anything could be, that to make a promise, for instance, is to create a moral claim on us in someone else. Many readers will perhaps say that they do not know this to be true. If so, I certainly cannot prove it to them; I can *only* ask them to reflect again, in the hope that they will ultimately agree that they also know it to be true."[1]

Prichard gives the same answer to the question that Ross does:

> "...suppose we came genuinely to doubt whether we ought, for example, to pay our debts, owing to a genuine doubt whether our previous conviction that we ought to do so is true, a doubt which can, in fact, only arise if we fail to remember the real nature of what we now call our past conviction. The *only* remedy lies in actually getting into a situation which occasions the obligation, or—if our imagination be strong enough—in imagining ourselves in that situation, and then letting our moral capacities of thinking [*i.e.*, our intuition] do their work."[2]

An intuitionist, if he is asked to justify his conviction that a moral proposition he intuits to be true really is true, must either admit that his conviction cannot be justified so is arbitrary or must appeal to some criterion of knowledge to support his stand. To justify himself rationally he has the logical alternatives of turning to either of two types of knowledge criterion. First, he can appeal to some knowledge criterion other than intuition and show that his intuition satisfies this

---

[2] Ross, *The Right and the Good*, p. 21, n. 1, (italics mine).
[3] Prichard, "Does Moral Philosophy Rest on a Mistake?" *Op. cit.*, pp. 36–37 (italics mine).

criterion. Although such an appeal is a logical possibility, the intuitionist cannot make use of it. For to accept it would be in substance to admit that he does not know that what he intuits to be true is true because he intuits it to be so but rather for some other reason. He would thus be abandoning his appeal to intuition as a criterion of moral knowledge so could no longer call himself an intuitionist. Furthermore, the new criterion to which he appealed would itself require justification and the same dilemma would arise again, and so on.

The only viable alternative for the intuitionist is to remain with intuition as his criterion of moral knowledge. And it is clear from the quotations I have given from Ross and Prichard that they would agree with me. If one does not recognize that promises as such ought to be kept, the *only* thing Ross can advise him to do is to reflect again (and again?) until he has the necessary intuition. Or if one doubts that an intuition he has had is veridical, Prichard writes, the *only* remedy is to have the intuition again.

Let us suppose, for the sake of argument, that we follow the advice the deontologists give and obtain the desired result. We do have an intuition of an obligation to perform a certain act. Can we now legitimately conclude that we *know* that we ought to do the act? Now the deontologists admit, as they must admit if they are to have a theory of moral knowledge, that false intuitions are a possibility. We are now assuming that we have an intuition that we ought to do a certain act and, faced with the possibility that our intuition may be false, are asking whether we can give some reason for believing it to be veridical. How can we go about this? To what can we appeal? The only answer that the intuitionists give (or can from the nature of the case give) is...intuition. To substantiate the fact that an intuition is veridical we must appeal to intuition. But it is the very appeal to intuition as a criterion of knowledge that is under challenge. The intuitionists' answer, therefore, begs the question.

On the basis of the arguments given we can conclude that it is logically impossible for intuitionism to justify itself as a theory of moral knowledge. Any attempt at justification either leads to an infinite regress or is question-begging. Anyone who bases his beliefs about what he ought to do on his intuitions must admit the possibility that his beliefs may be mistaken for he can give no reason that is capable of establishing that the beliefs are true. So he cannot conclude that he knows them to be true. Nothing that the intuitionists have to say, therefore, is incompatible with the truth of moral skepticism.

Once again our efforts to develop and defend an alternative to moral skepticism have ended in failure. But, even if we have not been able to rehabilitate intuitionism as a satisfactory theory of moral knowledge, we have accomplished something. We have discovered where its vulnerability lies. Since we know already the source of its strength, namely, its avoidance of the deductive fallacy, the possibility arises that we may be able to develop a theory which takes advantage of the strength of intuitionism and at the same time avoids its weakness. But what would such a theory be? In the next chapter I shall try to find an answer to this question.

CHAPTER VII

REASON AND DUTY

Before beginning my final attempt to find an alternative to moral skepticism, perhaps I should stipulate the requirements that any theory of moral knowledge must meet, if it is to be successful. Two are essential. First, it must enable us to make some statement asserting a moral obligation, whose truth we can justify without committing the deductive fallacy. To do this we must seek, in the manner of Prichard and the intuitionists, some moral proposition whose truth we can demonstrate to be self-evident. In demonstrating the self-evidence of this moral proposition, however, we must use a method that avoids begging any crucial questions, a feat which intuitionism is incapable of performing.

1. TWO NOTIONS OF SELF-EVIDENCE

The trouble with intuitionism, as we found in Chapter VI, is that it cannot justify the truth of the moral propositions it claims to be self-evident without always begging a vital question; namely, that what one intuits as true really is true. If we are to succeed in justifying moral knowledge through an appeal to self-evidence, then, we must turn to some other kind of self-evidence than that allegedly reached through intuition. But what other kind of self-evidence is there? Before answering this question, perhaps it would be best to clarify what we mean by self-evidence. To be self-evident a proposition must be true and its truth must be self-justifying. That is to say, it must be possible to establish the truth of the proposition directly, by appealing to the proposition itself. As an intuitionist might say, if a proposition is self-evident, it is so and can directly be apprehended to be so, simply by virtue of what it asserts. If we understand self-evidence in this way, then I think we can distinguish at least one other kind of self-evidence, different from the intuitive self-evidence we have talked about heretofore in this book. That is *logical* self-evidence, which can be defined as follows: A proposition is logically self-evident if its denial (logical contradictory) either is logically self-contradictory or implies a logical contradiction. Any such proposition would be self-evident because its truth could be directly demonstrated. For if its denial involves a contradiction then it must necessarily be true.

That logical self-evidence, as I have just defined it, is different from intuitive self-evidence is fairly clear. On the one hand, a proposition may be (held to be) intuitively self-evident without being logically self-evident. For instance, none of the propositions that I used as examples of alleged self-evident moral truths in the last chapter can be demonstrated to be true by showing that its denial involves a contradiction. On the other hand, moral intuition is irrelevant to logical self-evidence. If there are any propositions that assert a moral obligation whose truth is logically self-evident, then one can recognize the truth of these propositions even though he has no moral insight whatsoever. To establish the necessary truth of any such propositions (and hence the reality of moral knowledge) on the basis of their logical self-evidence, one would not have to make any appeal to distinctively moral considerations at all. On the contrary, the issue could be argued and decided on logical grounds alone.

Of course, it is one thing to explain what a logically self-evident moral proposition would be but quite another thing to show that any such propositions exist. However, I can see no other way of finding an answer to the problem of moral knowledge that avoids skepticism. The argument of the book so far has driven us inexorably to this point, for the objections that have destroyed the possible alternative defenses of moral knowledge can be avoided only by a theory that rests on an appeal to logical self-evidence. The conclusion seems inescapable that, *if* moral knowledge is possible, then there must be at least one proposition which asserts a moral obligation whose denial involves a contradiction. But is there such a proposition? I do not know. But I think there may be. At least I intend in this chapter to offer some propositions that may meet the necessary requirements and to defend these to the best of my abilities. Before I begin, however, I think I should meet some preliminary objections to my proposal. I shall raise three, discussing the first two briefly and the third at greater length. The reason I am raising these objections now is that, if they are cogent, they would rule out any possibility of my project's being successful from the very start. The discussion (which will occupy § 2) will take us out of the area of moral philosophy altogether, into general epistemology. The issues I shall raise are, I think, of great philosophical importance and really deserve much fuller consideration than the somewhat terse treatment that I give them here.

2. PRELIMINARY OBJECTIONS

A first objection to my proposal might be stated in this way: I am setting out to vindicate moral knowledge by finding a proposition that asserts a moral obligation whose denial involves a contradiction (is either itself self-contradictory or implies a contradiction). But such a proposition, if found, could not satisfy the requirements for knowledge because it would of necessity be a tautology. For any proposition whose denial involves a contradiction is necessarily tautologous.

It is quite true that some propositions whose denial involves a contradiction are tautologies. The classic example is the law of identity. That A must be A is true because the proposition "A is non-A" is self-contradictory. But the proposition "A is A" is the paradigm of tautologies. To establish the objection against my proposal, thus, it must be shown that all propositions whose denial involves a contradiction are, like the law of identity, also tautologies. How might this be shown? Obviously it would do no good to start examining propositions of the type in question individually, for there are an infinite number of them. And in any case the contention that all such propositions are tautologies is not meant to state an empirical generalization but rather a logical necessity. What it intends is that the propositions in question will be found universally to be tautologies because they *must* be tautologies. The necessity is logical and the argument *a priori*. Therefore, we must deal with it on logical grounds. To begin, we should note that the purpose of the contention is to establish that there can be no moral propositions that are logically necessary and at the same time non-tautologous. If it is to accomplish this purpose, it must itself be an informative (substantial) proposition, rather than simply a tautology. For no tautology could establish the kind of conclusion about other propositions that it is attempting to do. At the same time it must, to accomplish its goal, itself be logically necessary. If it is logically necessary, then its denial must involve a contradiction (since this is the criterion of logical necessity). But, if its denial involves a contradiction, then it itself, according to its own stipulation, must be a tautology. And, as we just pointed out, no tautology can accomplish the task this contention sets out to do. The objection, if it is to be any objection at all, must be a substantial proposition. But if it is a substantial proposition, it contradicts itself (by being a proposition that violates the very stipulation it lays down). Since the denial of a self-contradictory proposition is logically necessary, my original thesis that there are non-tautologous propositions whose denial involves a contradiction is demonstrably true. (It should be noted that I have demonstrated here only the general thesis that there must be substantial propositions whose denial involves a contradiction and not the specific thesis that any of these are moral propositions.)

A second charge that might be made against the method I have proposed for solving the problem of moral knowledge is that it falls into the same dilemma as intuitionism—being able to justify itself only by either an argument *ad infinitum* or by begging the question. The point may be put this way: I am proposing that the reality of moral knowledge can be established if a proposition asserting a moral obligation can be found which is logically self-evident. Such a proposal clearly rests on the assumption that logical self-evidence provides a satisfactory criterion of knowledge. But how can this assumption be justified? On what grounds can we justify our claim to know that a proposition which is logically self-evident is true? Either we must appeal for our justification to some other criterion of knowledge than logical self-evidence and then a further one and a further one and so on or we must simply assume that our criterion itself is an item of knowledge and hence beg the crucial question at issue.

My answer to this objection is that I can avoid the dilemma posed because the knowledge criterion, logical self-evidence, to which I appeal is self-justifying. Because it is self-justifying, we do not, on the one hand, need to appeal to another knowledge criterion to justify it, hence can avoid an infinite regress. But do we not, on the other hand, fall into the trap of begging the question by simply assuming the truth of our criterion from the outset? I should reply that a question can be begged *only* if there is a question *to be* begged. A theory can be called question-begging only if it can be shown that an alternative, incompatible theory on the issue is possible and is being ruled out of consideration arbitrarily. To beg the question one must first assume the truth of his own theory as against its possible alternatives and then, on this basis, carry on his argument. Now does my theory do that? It does so *only* if there are possible conflicting alternative theories which it rules out arbitrarily.

What I have proposed is that we can accept as an item of knowledge (because we can demonstrate it to be true) any moral proposition whose denial involves a contradiction. Now this proposal is a specification of the general theory that any proposition whose denial involves a contradiction is demonstrably true hence constitutes an item of knowledge. To show this general theory of knowledge to be question-begging, we must establish the possibility of an alternative incompatible theory, which it arbitrarily rules out of consideration. Now any such alternative theory would have to defend the thesis that a proposition whose denial involves a contradiction need not be demonstrably true. A proposition that is not demonstrably true, is one that may be false. Thus, to show that any proposition is not demonstrably true, one must establish the possibility of its falsehood and, by implication, the possibility of the truth of its denial. Is it possible that a proposition whose denial involves a contradiction could be false? If we assume it to be false, then it follows that its denial is true. But its denial involves a contradiction hence, logically, implies the truth of all propositions, including its own denial, which is our original proposition. The denial of our original proposition is either true or false; if it is false, our original proposition must be true, but if it is assumed to be true, our original proposition still must be true. In any case, then, our original proposition cannot be false so must be true; hence its denial cannot be true, and there is no possible alternative to our theory. The attempt to find an alternative to our theory forces us back logically to the theory itself, because the theory is logically undeniable. Since no real alternative opposed to it can exist, it begs no question by assuming its own truth. (Actually no assumption is being made because the theory is demonstrably true.) This is simply another way of putting the point I made earlier when I said that it is self-justifying. Hence it escapes the kind of criticism that I raised against the intuitionists' position at the end of Chapter VI.

The third objection to my proposal I shall consider at some length, not only because it would, if cogent, rule out any possibility of my making my case but also because it represents a view that I think a great many philosophers take very seriously indeed. If I am to succeed in establishing the reality of moral knowledge by discovering a moral proposition that is logically self-evident, I must produce a proposition that possesses two characteristics: (1) It must be a substantial proposition, rather than a tautology. This is true because it asserts a moral obligation and no mere tautology can do that. (2) It must be logically necessary. This characteristic simply puts in formal terms the requirement that it be logically self-evident. Now, the criticism runs, I shall never be able to discover such a proposition because no proposition satisfying both of these two requirements can exist. To seek for a proposition that is at once both substantial and logically necessary is to attempt the impossible. It should be noted that the objection is quite general, applying to all possible propositions and not simply to moral propositions. Because there can be no substantial, logically necessary propositions, *a fortiori* there can be none which asserts a moral obligation.

It is quite clear that this objection, if sound, is conclusive. One point, however, should be noted at the outset; that, if this criticism based on the denial of substantial, logically necessary propositions is to destroy my hypothesis, that denial must itself be considered to be a theory. What I mean is that the denial must be capable of propositional formulation. To attack my proposal on this point, a critic must accept the truth of the proposition (which is the denial of my thesis) "No substantial propositions are logically necessary." If this proposition is true, then my endeavor is futile and must be abandoned; however, if it can be shown to be not true, then I can disregard the objection and proceed with my investigation.

What I shall do in the next several pages is to try to reach a judgment regarding the truth of the proposition "No substantial propositions are logically necessary." As a beginning toward this end I shall attempt to determine how the proposition itself ought properly to be classified. In the first place, is it a substantial proposition or is it simply a tautology? Let us begin with the second alternative, assuming it to be a tautology. If it is a tautology, it is non-informative or vacuous. It provides us with no information about anything. Its truth as a tautology is conventional, resting on someone's arbitrary definition of the terms it contains. Because it does not provide us with information about anything, there is nothing in the nature of things that forces us to accept it. Granted that if one accepts it, he then cannot deny it or its logical implications without contradiction, there is no theoretical reason forcing anyone to accept it. He may, or may not, accept the particular conventional definitions of the terms it contains that make it a tautology. And if he does not do so, then he is quite free to multiply substantial, logically necessary propositions at will—without restraint from the person who does accept it as a conventional tautology. All that the conventionalist could say to him would be "If you do that you are violating the definitions I have given of the terms in the proposition." But what the conventionalist must say, if he is to make his case against the existence of substantial, logically necessary propositions, is "You cannot violate the definitions I have given of these terms." This, however, he could not say if the proposition is a tautology. For to do so would be to deny that its truth rests on conventional definitions.

Furthermore, if the proposition is assumed to be a tautology, then any conclusions logically derived from it would, like it, have to be vacuous, conveying no information about anything. For from a tautology only further tautologies, and never substantial propositions, can be logically derived. Now the objective of the theory we are examining (as far as our present purposes are concerned) is to rule out the possibility *a fortiori* of substantial, logically necessary *moral* propositions. However, if the proposition "No substantial propositions are logically necessary" is considered to be a tautology, then the proposition, which follows logically from it, "No substantial moral propositions are logically necessary" is equally a tautology. As such it is subject to the same limitations as the original. Specifically, it can never prohibit anyone from producing substantial, logically necessary moral propositions. For these reasons, the interpretation of the theory in question as a tautology must be abandoned in favor of its alternative. So we can conclude that the proposition "No substantial propositions are logically necessary," if it is to have any success in eliminating the possibility of substantial, logically necessary moral propositions, must itself be considered to be a substantial proposition.

Accepting the fact that the proposition we are considering is itself substantial, we must now try to decide how its truth might be established. Two alternative ways of substantiating it are possible— empirical confirmation or logical demonstration. Is the proposition, once again remembering the objective it sets out to accomplish, to be construed as an empirical generalization or as a logical truth? There are two major objections to its classification as an empirical generalization. In the first place, if it were so classified, it would be only general, not universal. All that it could warrant anyone's saying would be "No substantial propositions have yet been discovered which have been logically necessary as well." What the critic could not say—and what he must say if he is to make his case against me—is "No substantial propositions *can be* logically necessary." If the proposition were simply an empirical generalization, the way would be left open for anyone to embark on the kind of quest that I am proposing for this chapter; namely, the attempt to discover a proposition that is at once both substantial and logically necessary. But a more general criticism of the interpretation of the proposition in question as an empirical generalization is the fact that it is simply not empirical at all. For a proposition to qualify as empirical, it must deal with an empirical subject-matter. That is to say, the truth of what it asserts must be capable in principle of confirmation by means of sense observation. Now the subject matter of the proposition under examination is "propositions" and "logical necessity" and both are types of entity or attribute that are intrinsically unobservable. (I shall not here go into the somewhat complex argument necessary to defend this point but will assume it to be accepted.) To establish the truth of the proposition, therefore, one cannot appeal to any empirical evidence; rather he must base his case on logical considerations alone. If it is a truth at all, this proposition must be a logical truth. In other words, if it is true it is so because it is logically necessary. But how can it be shown to be logically necessary? Only by showing that its denial is self-contradictory (or implies a contradiction). So we must investigate the logical necessity and logical self-contradictoriness of both this proposition and its denial.

Let us begin with the proposition we have been examining. Is it logically necessary or is it logically self-contradictory? It states that no substantial propositions are logically necessary but we have discovered that, in order to establish this thesis and thus prevent me from carrying out my proposal, it must itself be at once both substantial and logically necessary. Thus it must itself be an example of a kind of proposition that it says cannot exist. In other words, it is self-contradictory, necessarily affirming (by its own example) the very existence of what it denies. So we can conclude on logical grounds alone that, because this proposition is self-contradictory, its denial is logically necessary. Thus the proposition (which is the logical denial of the proposition we have been examining) "Some substantial propositions are logically necessary" or "Propositions which are at once both substantial and logically necessary do exist" is necessarily true. This proposition, being the logical denial of a substantial proposition, must be substantial as well, so we have demonstrated the existence of a proposition which is both substantial and logically necessary; namely, the proposition which affirms the necessary existence of substantial, logically necessary propositions. (It should be noted that the cogency of this demonstration does not depend on the contingent question of whether anyone in fact has denied the existence of substantial, logically necessary propositions; to establish the conclusion I have reached it is sufficient to show that such a denial, when formulated, leads logically to a self-contradiction.)

My purpose in the argument above has been to eliminate the objection to my proposal that, because there can be no substantial, logically necessary propositions, *a fortiori* there can be none which asserts a moral obligation. We are now in a position to assert without qualification that we know that there are substantial propositions whose truth is logically necessary. However, I am not confident that everyone who reads this will agree with my conclusion. The conviction that propositions cannot be both substantial and logically necessary is deeply engrained, particularly among contemporary philosophers. It is a view that I once accepted myself, until I was forced by the weight of the argument to give it up in favor of the position I am advocating here. I now believe that there are substantial, logically necessary propositions because there must be. To convince others, all that I can do is to present the arguments and rest my case.

But even if the conclusion I have reached is true, how far does it take us? Unfortunately, not very far. For the crucial question still lies waiting to be answered: Can we establish the fact that, included among those propositions that are at once both substantial and logically necessary, there is *any* that asserts a moral obligation? It is to this issue that I shall devote the remainder of the chapter. Before I begin, however, I should like to make a few summary and introductory remarks. I have become convinced of three things. First, if moral knowledge is to be vindicated, there *must* be a proposition that asserts a moral obligation which is necessarily true. If there is no such proposition, the moral skeptics are correct; these are the only alternatives. Secondly, I have a strong conviction that there is such a proposition. For I believe that at least some of the basic moral tenets of mankind do rest on a rational foundation. But, finally, I am not completely satisfied with the case I make for the position to which I am committing myself. I realize that my argument will fall short in many ways but I hope that it may suggest to others a fruitful approach toward a solution to the problem of moral knowledge. If this should prove true, I shall be more than satisfied with what I have done.

3. DUTY AND GOOD REASONS

To begin my argument, I should like to take up a point that I raised in the first chapter of the book (1.3). This concerns the nature of duty or moral obligation. At that time I suggested that a main reason why most traditional moral philosophers have failed in their attempts to solve the problem of moral knowledge is that they have accepted uncritically certain of our ordinary moral expressions, and thus have been forced to seek answers to problems that, besides being unreal, cannot be solved. To be specific, they have noted that in our ordinary discourse we make substantives of such terms as "obligation" and "duty," saying, for example, "I have an obligation to do act X" or "It is my duty to do act X." The traditional moral philosopher, taking this kind of language at its face-value, assumes that a duty is some kind of *thing* which, it is alleged, a person can *have*. Now, such a philosopher argues, if duty is thought of as some kind of thing, then, to refute the skeptics, it is necessary to establish that it really does exist (*i.e.*, that it is like a horse rather than a unicorn). So he tries desperately to show that obligations exist (or are "real") and that people have them. But all of his arguments prove unconvincing. A major reason for his failure, I believe, lies in the fact that he has based his case on a false analogy derived from his uncritical acceptance of ordinary usage. I am convinced that this traditional approach to the problem must be abandoned and that, instead of basing our theory on the language people actually use in their ordinary moral discourse, we must shift our perspective, approaching the issue from an examination of the situations in which they use this kind of language and the reasons why they do so.

Neither morality nor moral language exists in a vacuum. Rather both represent a distinctively human response to certain situations that people, no matter when or where they may live, have to face. The root source of both moral judgment and moral activity is conflict. Human beings, like other animals, are creatures of desire. They have various needs and inclinations, which they naturally seek to satisfy. In their attempts to do so, however, they find themselves in conflict with other humans, who are seeking the satisfaction of their own wants and desires. When such conflicts of interest occur, two methods of resolution are possible—force (or cunning) and rational adjudication. The first method is universal among animals; because they are not simply creatures of desire but have the capacity for reason as well, the second is possible for men. By rational adjudication of a conflict of interests I mean something like this: If two people find themselves desiring the same object, each one, instead of trying to obtain that object by any methods he can lay his hands to without regard to the desires and wishes of the other, desists from action to consider what reasons he can advance to justify his gaining the object in dispute. When each has presented his case the one whose arguments are the weaker, if he responds rationally, will waive his claim in favor of the other. Whether or not human beings very often act in such a rational way, they are capable of doing so. They are the one kind of creature we know that can adjudicate the conflicts into which their opposed desires lead them by the use of reason. It is this capacity which makes men capable of morality. If no one ever found himself desiring an object that someone else wanted too or if he could not dispassionately review the strength of the reasons he and the other person had for gaining the object and then act accordingly, human life could have no moral dimension.

Our moral concepts and our moral language have their ultimate source in these basic conditions of human life and capacities of man. They can be made intelligible only when they are understood in terms of this context, which gives them their significance. Interpreted from this new perspective, when someone says "I have a duty to do that act," he does not mean that he possesses some unique, indefinable entity, a duty, but rather that he cannot justify his not doing the act, or that he has no good reasons for not doing it. It might be objected that I am putting ideas into the mind of the ordinary user of moral language that are simply not to be found there. I admit that the average person probably is not explicitly aware of just what he means, or is intending to convey or imply, when he ascribes moral obligations, or uses moral language in general. In fact he would probably, if asked to explain what he meant, either shrug his shoulders at the thought that anyone should need an explanation of anything so obvious or else, if he tried to answer, soon be reduced to complete confusion. But even the most unphilosophical person, I am inclined to believe, when he uses moral language seriously, is at least dimly aware that he is concerned with the problem of providing some justification for action and when, for example, he says of some act a person has done "He ought not to have done that," he would, if pressed, agree that his reason for making this judgment was in part his conviction that the person who had done the act could not justify his doing it. (At least one other element must be taken into consideration; I shall discuss it later.)

I shall take the interpretation I have just given of the moral concepts with which we are here concerned as the basis from which to attack the problem of moral knowledge. My reasons for doing so are two: (1) As I have just indicated, I think this interpretation gets behind the screen of our ordinary usage to the significant meanings this usage is meant to convey and (2) I believe that my interpretation can lead to a satisfactory solution to the problem of moral knowledge. For the remainder of the chapter I shall address myself to the second point. (I shall continue to use ordinary expressions like "duty" and "obligation" even though I think they have misled moral philosophers. It should be remembered that, whenever I do use them, I am understanding them in terms of the interpretation I have just given.)

According to the hypothesis I have advanced, to hold that a person has a duty or a moral obligation to do a certain act is to imply that he has no good reasons to give for not doing it and to hold that he has a duty or obligation not to do it is to imply that he has no good reasons to give for doing it. It follows, thus, that we shall be able to demonstrate that a person has a duty to do some given act, and thus to establish the existence of moral knowledge, if we can demonstrate that the reasons he has to give for not doing it are not good reasons (and to demonstrate that he has a duty not to do the act if we can demonstrate that the reasons he has to give for doing it are not good reasons). But how could we demonstrate this last point? How could we prove that a reason given for doing a certain act is not a good reason (*i.e.*, cannot justify doing that act)? The answer to these questions should be clear from what I have said earlier in the chapter. What we must do is to show that the reason given as a reason for doing the act is either self-contradictory or implies a contradiction. One way in which we can do this, and the way with which I shall be concerned, is to show that the reason given for doing the act is equally a reason for not doing it. Such a reason cannot be a *good* reason for doing the act in question because, being equally a reason for not doing it, it is *no* reason for doing the act at all. The contradiction implied by such a reason may be made more clear by pointing out that, if the reason given for doing the act is equally a reason for not doing it, then both the proposition "Reason so-and-so is a reason for doing act X" and the proposition "Reason so-and-so is a reason for not doing act X" would be true. But each denies what the other asserts. Such a reason, therefore, cannot be used to justify performance of the act.

4. A MORAL AXIOM

If we take the conclusions of the last section and put them together in a single proposition, we should be able to get an ascription of duty or a moral injunction, which, because it is logically self-evident, can justifiably be called a moral axiom. I shall state this proposition as follows: "One ought never to do an act having negative moral effects if his reason for doing the act is equally a reason for not doing it." In alternative formulations we can say that one has a duty or moral obligation not to do such an act or that performance of the act is immoral.

Having stated what I have ventured to call a moral axiom, perhaps the first thing I should do is to try to make its meaning as clear as I can. The only part of my proposition that requires elucidation, I believe, is the phrase "negative moral effects." An act has negative effects if its consequences affect people (or even a single person) other than the agent adversely—that is, decrease their happiness, hinder their welfare, or run counter to their interests. No matter what other consequences, good or bad, the act may have, if it in any way hurts other people, then it has negative moral effects, as I am using that term. I shall use the term "negative moral effects" in another, slightly less obvious but equally important sense. On this usage an act has negative moral effects if its consequences affect a limited number of people, which may include the agent, favorably. Although the consequences of the act here are not directly negative, they are so indirectly in that the individuals who do not share in them miss out on the increase of happiness, promotion of welfare, or augmentation of interests enjoyed by those who do. By this interpretation of the term "negative moral effects" I wish to imply that one ought never to do an act which discriminates in favor of an individual or a limited group of people at the expense of the rest if his reason for doing it is equally a reason for not doing it. Although the first meaning I give to "negative moral effects" probably applies to acts which are most dramatically and unequivocally immoral, the second, I think, applies much more to the minor immoralities that most of us indulge in most frequently.

The emphasis that I have put on the effects of an act on people other than the agent, whether direct or indirect, is essential to my argument. As I indicated in the last section, morality is a phenomenon of social life, springing out of the active relationships between each individual and his fellows. To have any moral significance an act must, either directly or indirectly, have social consequences. If a person performs some act that hurts only himself, and his reason for doing it is equally a reason for his not doing it, we would not say that he had acted immorally but rather gratuitously or foolishly. (Of course, if the act helped only himself, we would call it immoral, on the basis of my second interpretation of "negative moral effects.") If we then went on to say that the person ought not to have done the act, the "ought" in our judgment would be the prudential, not the moral "ought." In a world in which there were no other persons or none whose wants and desires came into conflict with my own, there would be no meaning in attributing moral obligations to me. I could with complete moral license do what I wanted to do.

It follows from what I have just said that I do not believe that there are any such things as "duties to oneself." Many moral philosophers would disagree with me here, using the expression to refer to the alleged duty one has so to govern his behavior that he will not perform any act whose consequences will cause him some serious future harm. I think it is worth noting that those who hold this view usually explain what they mean by such a duty by saying that it is a duty which our "present self" owes to our "future self." Thus implicitly they acknowledge that moral obligation implies a social relationship, which they impart into a personal situation by dividing the individual in question into two selves, one of whom owes a duty to the other. In favor of the theory I think it must be acknowledged that people need to be reminded that they ought to consider the effects of what they do on their own future welfare so that they will not be tempted into hasty actions detrimental to their long-range interests; and further, that the necessity for such foresight can be dramatized by casting the figure of oneself at some future time in the form of an independent person whose claims should be duly considered. But, because one's future self, no matter in what way it may differ from one's present self, is still the same person (only changed and grown older) rather than someone else, I should argue that the "duties" we owe to that self do not represent moral obligations but "counsels of prudence." The "ought," in other words, is the prudential rather than the moral "ought."

The question might be raised why I have inserted the notion of "negative moral effects" into my moral injunction. Would the injunction not be equally axiomatic if it read simply: "One ought never to do an act if his reason for doing the act is equally a reason for not doing it"? It is true that the injunction, as I have now formulated it, would be axiomatic but it would state only a logical and not a moral injunction. The "ought" in it, in other words, would be a logical, not a moral "ought." To have moral content the injunction must relate the act to the human situation and the relationships between men that give rise to morality and moral judgments. I have used the concept of "negative moral effects" to provide that relationship.

I have called my moral injunction an axiom, on the grounds that it is logically self-evident. But it might be argued that I have not stated in it a duty that holds good universally and necessarily (which it must do if the injunction is to be logically self-evident), because there are situations in which the obligation does not hold. Specifically, we owe nothing to a person who releases us from our normal obligation to him. If we consider doing an act for which we have no justification that will hurt another, the moral injunction against so acting collapses if the other person gives us permission to do the act anyway. This might happen in situations in which the person decided to sacrifice his own welfare, say, for some cause.

The objection can, I think, be met in either of two ways. In the first place, it could be argued that the injunction still holds in situations of the type I have suggested. For no one can release us from our obligation to him. I am inclined myself not to take this line, although I do not see that it can be ruled completely out of consideration. But if one admits, as I would do, that we can release others from their obligation to us, I think it is possible to accommodate this admission to my moral injunction. I could, for example, add a qualification to my moral axiom, to the effect that, for an act to be immoral, it must not only have negative moral effects but the person who would suffer these effects must also be unwilling to do so. The injunction might then read "One ought never to do an act having negative moral effects against the will of those suffering these effects if his reason for doing the act is equally a reason for not doing it." Or I could argue that, in a situation in which the victim of my proposed action himself accepts the consequences (*i.e.*, is willing to suffer them), then what would normally be called negative moral effects are in this situation no longer negative for they are the effects that the other person desires. I think I could preserve the self-evidence of my injunction by either type of answer. However, the objection brings out a point that might otherwise be overlooked; namely, that my injunction does assume that people are not ordinarily willing to have their happiness or welfare violated by the activities of others. Nevertheless, in some instances they may be glad to sacrifice that happiness.

One other problem arising out of my formulation of the moral injunction should be considered. The injunction could be stated in either of two ways, one strong and one weak. I have chosen the stronger form. The difference between the two is this. My formulation "One ought never to do an act having negative moral effects if his reason for doing it is equally a reason for not doing it" implies that an act is immoral, even though it *could* be rationally justified, if the reason the agent *actually* has for doing it cannot provide such a justification. The weaker version would run "One ought never to do an act having negative moral effects if he can give no reason for doing it that would not equally be a reason for not doing it." This second version is the weaker of the two because it would rule out fewer acts as immoral for, logically, every act judged immoral by its standard would be immoral by the standard of the first formulation but some acts judged immoral by the first formulation could be morally justified on its terms.

I have two main reasons for choosing the stronger of the two formulations of the injunction. In the first place, I think that it reflects more closely than the other the basis on which we ordinarily make our moral judgments. This fact can be seen most clearly by considering our evaluations of acts people have done. If, after considering some accomplished act, we conclude that it was immoral on the grounds that its performance could not be rationally justified, we do so because we are convinced that the reasons the agent actually had for doing it could not justify it and not that no justifying reasons could possibly be given for it. Whether or not such reasons could be found, the fact that they were not in fact operative in this instance is sufficient for us to judge the act immoral. Secondly, if the weaker formulation is accepted, there is a serious question about the possibility of judging any act immoral. For are there any acts for whose performance *no* reason can be found that would not equally be a reason for their non-performance? I do not see any way of giving a general answer to this question that would be definitive; however, I think I could find some reason for doing any act that anyone might suggest to me that would not equally be a reason for not doing it. If this is possible, then not one of those acts could, on the weaker formulation, be judged immoral. Yet I think that any one of these acts would normally be considered immoral, if it had negative moral effects and were done by a person for a reason that he could not show to be capable of justifying his doing it.

It is my contention that any contemplated act that has the characteristics set forth in the stronger formulation of the moral injunction, as I have explained it, provides a *sufficient* condition for the ascription of a moral obligation. If a person considers doing some act that has negative moral effects for a reason that would equally serve as a reason for his not doing it, we can conclude that he always has a duty not to do that act. But does the proposed performance of such an act constitute a *necessary* condition for the ascription of a moral obligation as well? Or can it ever be legitimately asserted that a person has a duty not to do a certain act even though it cannot be shown that the reason he has for doing the act would equally be a reason for his not doing it? I am not sure. Certainly some moral philosophers would contend that fulfilment of the conditions of my injunction, if made a necessary condition for the ascription of a moral obligation, would unduly limit morality. Many of the acts that we believe people ought not to do, they would argue, do not satisfy the conditions I have set up. Must we therefore conclude that they are morally at liberty to do them? I would try to answer this point in three ways. First, it may turn out that the number of kinds of acts commonly assumed to be immoral that fail to meet my conditions is not so great as it may at first glance appear to be. The defense of this supposition, however, must await the full elaboration of the theory I am developing. Secondly, it must be remembered that I am trying to develop a theory of moral obligation that I can defend as representing knowledge. Now, there may well be many things, particularly in the realm of morals, that are true but that we cannot demonstrate to be true. If I am to defend my position successfully, I must try to stick strictly to those things that I can demonstrate to be true. By doing so I almost surely will leave out other things that are in fact true. If so, this is a loss that I can see no way of avoiding. Finally, if I do succeed in demonstrating that satisfaction by an act of the conditions of my injunction constitutes a sufficient condition for the ascription of a moral obligation, whether or not it constitutes a necessary condition as well, I shall have demonstrated the truth of a moral proposition. Thus I will have accomplished the goal which I have set for myself, a successful defense of the reality of moral knowledge against the attacks of the skeptics.

Here, however, a serious objection can be raised. Let us assume, for purposes of argument, that my moral injunction is logically self-evident. The injunction, being logically self-evident, is an item of knowledge. But is it an item of *moral* knowledge? Although it lays down a condition in terms of which we can judge an act immoral, it does not itself stipulate that any act we might do is in fact immoral. Perhaps there are no acts that anyone has ever done or will ever do that satisfy the conditions it lays down. If this is true, then we cannot demonstrate of any act that has ever been done or will ever be done that the agent ought not to have done it. What we shall have produced is a criterion for a demonstrably true ascription of moral obligation but not an ascription of a moral obligation that we can demonstrate to be true. And it is the latter that we must produce. To overcome this deficiency, we must advance to the second stage in the argument. This will consist in showing that my moral injunction is not simply a theoretical formulation but has practical applicability as well. To establish this point, I shall give examples of actual or possible actions that, because they fulfil the conditions laid down in my injunction, are immoral—acts that the agent ought not to have done.

5. A STORY

There is a story that comes out of the first World War, about a unit of the French army on the Western Front.[1] According to the story this unit was forced by enemy pressure to retire from its defense position to a new line. The commander of the unit ordered his troops to assemble and told the men that the new defense line must be held at all costs because ultimate victory depended on it. He then ordered his men to count off by tens, after which he called each tenth man out of formation and had him shot. The remainder were sent into the new line, which held firm. The commander, however, was later court-martialled by the French army.

Most people, when they first hear this story, are shocked. They feel that the French commander's action was highly immoral. And further reflection generally confirms their initial response. For few people, no matter how long they have considered the case, would be willing to grant that the commander's action could be defended morally. The judgment of the moral consciousness seems to be quite clear here; intuitively most people just "know" the act to be wrong. But is their intuition sound? I think that it is and shall try to defend it by showing that the commander's action was demonstrably immoral.

My argument rests on a consideration of two points: the reason why

---

[1] My historian friends assure me that the story is apocryphal; nevertheless it persists. Suetonius tells a somewhat similar story about the military career of Caesar Augustus so perhaps it is just one of those legends that are brought up-to-date by each generation. That the event I describe ever actually occurred is, after all, not crucial to my argument.

the commander executed one-tenth of his troops and the reason why he executed the tenth that he did. The explanation of the first point is fairly clear. Committed to holding the new defense line, he hit on a plan that he was convinced would be successful and put it into operation. And he was right. The remaining ninety percent of his men held fast whereas the original force may well have broken as they had before. His reason for executing a tenth of his troops, thus, was to hold the defense line against the enemy. Turning to the second point, Why did the commander execute the tenth that he did? His answer to this question would be the same as to the first—he executed them in order to hold the defense line. But, does this answer really meet the point? Granted that it answers the question, Why did he execute a tenth of his troops? does it answer the question, Why did he execute every tenth man in line, *beginning* with number 10? It does so only if the execution of every tenth man in line, beginning with the *tenth* one, would fulfil his purpose, but the execution of a tenth of his troops, chosen *in any other* way than this, would not. But this is not so. The men selected for execution were unique in his command *only* in the fact that they stood tenth, twentieth, thirtieth, and so on, in line. The commander could have used the same plan with equal success but, instead of calling men numbers 10, 20, 30 ..., out of line for execution, could have called men numbers 9, 19, 29 ..., or 8, 18, 28 ..., and so on. *Any* tenth of his forces so chosen would have served his purposes *equally* well. In other words, the commander's reason for doing the act he did is equally as good a reason for his doing a large number of alternative acts. But this is to imply that his reason for doing the act is equally a reason for his not doing it. Thus his act satisfies the conditions of the moral injunction I have set up. It is an act having negative moral effects and his reason for doing it is equally a reason for his not doing it. The act is therefore immoral, one that he ought not to have done. It might be added that, even though any one of the alternative acts which I have suggested that the commander could have done would have served his purposes equally as well as the one he did, none could be justified morally. For all suffer from exactly the same defect as the act he actually did.

6. ELABORATION AND COMMENTS

I believe that the explanation I have just given of why the French commander's action was immoral provides a reasonably accurate statement of the grounds on which the average person would condemn what he did. When such a person says that he simply knows the act to be wrong, he is not appealing to direct intuition, in the sense that his "knowledge" is a flash of insight that exists in a vacuum, without any relationship to his consideration of the context in which the act he is judging has taken place. On the contrary, he would have reasons to give in support of his "intuition," although he might find some difficulty in putting these into words. If he were able to articulate his reasons, I think that he would put most stress on the following points. First, the act was extreme. Not only did the commander hurt his victims, but he inflicted on them what is generally felt to be the greatest harm a human being can suffer—loss of his life. Secondly, he did it against their will. The men were not asked if they would sacrifice their lives nor even told that they were to die; they were just lined up and shot. It might be argued that these men were soldiers and, as such, had tacitly consented to accept whatever the vicissitudes of war should bring. The argument is good, but only up to a point. Had the men been killed in combat they would have had no grounds for complaint. For the chance of death on the battlefield is a risk one accepts when he puts on a uniform in time of war. But to be summarily shot by one's commanding officer is not included in the commitment a soldier makes on enlistment. That the French army agreed on this point is implied by their bringing the commander before a court-martial. Finally, the act was completely arbitrary. This incident from the world war did not mark the first time soldiers had been executed by their commanders. But in other cases presumably the men in question were executed for a reason; they had fallen asleep on watch, been guilty of gross coward-ice, and so on. They had done something to deserve punishment. However, in the case we are concerned with the men who were shot had done nothing to deserve being *singled out* for punishment. The only thing that set them apart from the remaining ninety percent of their group was the fact that they were standing at the fatal spots in the line when the count was taken. It is primarily for reasons like these that the ordinary person, whether or not he consciously thought them through, would hold the conviction, which he might himself think to be directly and intuitively apparent, that the act in question was immoral. What I am arguing is that these reasons, besides furnishing the psychological basis for an apparently direct intuition condemning the act, provide as well a logical basis for a demonstrably certain judgment that the act ought not to have been done.

What have I been trying to do in the last paragraph? It might appear that I have been attempting to give strength to my theory by arguing that the judgment it makes in the case in question is supported by moral intuition. My intent is just the opposite. What I am suggesting is this. Although it is impossible to justify any moral judgment as an item of knowledge by an appeal to intuition, nevertheless our moral intuitions are by no means wholly irrational or arbitrary. Although many of the moral convictions people have held most strongly and for long periods of time cannot be defended against critical attack, others on examination prove themselves to be expressions of principles whose truth can be demonstrated. I do not know of any way of providing an easy method of deciding whether any given alleged intuitive moral truth does or does not have a rational foundation. All that I can suggest is that each individual one would have to be examined with great care and thoroughness and emphasize that the method that must be employed in testing it, if it is to be validated as an item of knowledge, cannot involve any appeal to some other alleged intuition, but must hold strictly to the attempt to determine whether or not its truth can be logically demonstrated.

But my belief that my condemnation of the commander's act, on the grounds that the reason he had for doing it could never justify his doing it, would be accepted by those who base their moral judgments on intuition might be challenged. I can well imagine an intuitionist asserting that the commander was morally justified in what he did and then supporting his judgment by arguing that anyone who considers the *entire* situation in which the act occurred will be forced to agree with him. What those intuitionists who would condemn the commander have failed to consider sufficiently, he could add, is the fact that the act was necessary to insure stabilization of the battle line, which in turn contributed to victory in the campaign and eventually in the war. The act unquestionably was extreme but, because it provided the only possible way to achieve an over-riding goal, it was morally justified. In these circumstances the end clearly justified the means. To my logical argument that the consequences to which the act led could not justify its performance because the commander could have realized the same consequences by the arbitrary execution of *any* tenth of his troops, the objector might reply by turning the tables on me, arguing that, because the success of the commander's tactic depended on the act's being done arbitrarily, he would have been equally justified morally no matter *which* tenth of his men he had selected for execution.

We seem to be caught in a dilemma here. If we assume (for purposes of argument) that an arbitrary act of the kind done was the *only* device capable of rallying the remaining troops to stand fast and that stabilization of the line was essential to gain final victory—both, of course, very large assumptions—then we seem forced to admit that the commander had a reason (and perhaps even a good one) for acting arbitrarily. But when we examine the specific act that he did we find that the reason just given to justify performance of an arbitrary act cannot justify performance of *this particular* arbitrary act. However, it is an act like this (one in which a portion of the troops are arbitrarily executed) that the reason does appear to justify. The commander seems to be in the peculiar position of being able to give a reason for arbitrarily executing a tenth of his troops, but not being able to give a reason for arbitrarily executing any given tenth of them.

I think there is one way out of this dilemma, but only one. Even if we admit, for purposes of argument, that the only way in which the commander could secure a stabilized battle line was through the arbitrary execution of a tenth of his troops, we must remember that the act that we are concerned with justifying here is not correctly described simply as his execution of a tenth of his troops but rather as his execution of a *particular* tenth of these men. It is the killing of a certain, specific, nameable group of human beings, who together constitute a tenth of his whole unit, that the commander's reason *must* justify. But the reason being advanced now will not justify that act because the execution of the particular men who were killed was not necessary to the realization of the end which is held to justify the act, for that end could equally well have been gained by the execution of any tenth of his troops. The same argument would hold true, of course, no matter which specific tenth of his men, selected arbitrarily, he had chosen for execution. Therefore, the attempt of a defender of the commander to turn the tables on me by the claim that he would have been justified no matter which tenth of his men he had arbitrarily chosen for execution, I believe, breaks down. In the situation I have been portraying, the end to be achieved cannot justify the means that were actually used.

This is the case against the commander. Because he had no reason to give that would justify his doing the act he did, he had no good reason for doing it; therefore, because it had negative moral effects, he ought not to have done it.

The commander's reason could not justify his act. That, I believe, is clear. This does not mean, however, that he should be condemned without qualification. For he could plead extenuating circumstances, arguing that the intent behind his act was a worthy one. Believing that all other considerations should be subordinated to the goal of military victory, he acted accordingly. For him that single end was sufficient to justify any means. That it could not justify the means he chose is a fact that he, as a person entrusted with military command over others, should have been expected to realize. Yet, that he did not realize it in the circumstances is perhaps understandable. In judging this case, therefore, we must distinguish between the act and the agent. The act itself was indefensible, hence immoral. The agent, however, should not be judged so harshly. For we should weigh against his moral culpability the fact that his intent in acting, unlike his act, was to some degree morally defensible.

Before leaving this particular example I should like to discuss one other objection that might be raised against my conclusion. The argument, which rests on the assumption (which I have already criticized) that the only act capable of producing the result the commander sought was the act he did, is this: The commander is caught in a moral dilemma. One set of considerations of acknowledged moral weight justify the act; another set of equal weight condemn it. Because the two sets of considerations balance each other off, there are no rational grounds on which he can make a decision. A situation posing such an irresolvable dilemma cannot be judged on moral terms so he is free to do whatever he pleases, without any moral censure of his act.

I think I have already met this objection in my earlier discussion. The decisive argument against it is that the opposed moral considerations are not, as it supposes, of equal weight. For no appeal to consequences can ever give the commander a good reason for doing the act he did. However, the objection raises two general points that are worth comment: (1) Does the fact that a person finds himself caught in a moral dilemma justify him in acting without regard to moral considerations? and (2) Is anyone ever trapped in an inescapable moral dilemma? Both of these questions seem to me to be very difficult to answer. To handle the first I think that it is necessary to make a distinction, of the type I have made already in connection with the commander's case, between the act and the agent. The fact that a person is caught in an inescapable moral dilemma and so commits an immoral act does not, as far as I can see, alter the immoral nature of the act he does. If the act is immoral it is so because it is what it is and its nature is not altered by the fact that the agent finds himself compelled to commit it. However, we may censure an act and spare the agent. If he has *no* alternative, then we do not blame him for what he does. In a situation of this kind are found the ingredients of tragedy. The example that comes to mind immediately is Sophocles' *Antigone*, in which both protagonists find themselves trapped in moral dilemmas. Antigone's predicament is the more clear-cut. She is caught between the moral demand made on her by the edict of the king, on the one side, and that founded on her religious beliefs, on the other. If she buries Polynices, she deliberately flouts the law; if she leaves him unburied, she violates her own (and the city's) religion. In making her choice she precipitated a series of events which culminated inevitably in tragedy.

The tragedy of Antigone raises naturally the second question, Is anyone ever really trapped in a moral dilemma that is absolutely inescapable? I am not sure that any definitive answer can be given to this question. Some philosophers would disagree with me here because they have a ready *a priori* answer. On the assumption—usually, but not always, based on theological grounds—that the universe must be morally rational, they conclude that there can be no such moral dilemmas. It is, I suppose, just possible that they are right. If so, the moral surds that we think we find in human existence are merely apparent and not real. But in the absence of any conclusive arguments in favor of their view, I prefer to accept the evidence of experience as a good reason for doubting the alleged universal moral rationality that such philosophers assert.

The problems involved in the two questions I have just raised could be discussed indefinitely. However, I leave them with only this very cursory treatment, to turn to still another criticism of my position but one of a nature quite different from those I have been considering. The problem may be put in this way: I have said that we can know that a person ought not to do an act having negative moral effects if his reason for doing it is equally a reason for not doing it. But this thesis, which purports to establish the existence of moral knowledge, rests on a questionable assumption; namely, that we can know what a person's reason for doing an act is. Now is this really possible? Certainly we can be reasonably sure, from the way the person acts or from the way in which he justifies his action, what his reason for doing it is. In the example we have been using, it is fair to assume that the French commander's reason for executing a tenth of his troops was to stabilize the battle line. However, can we say for certain that this was his *real* reason for doing the act? Can we ever make such a statement about anyone's acts? And if we cannot, how can we talk of moral knowledge?

I think that we must always admit the possibility, even though it be a remote one, of being mistaken about the reasons a person has for what he does. There simply is no way of our obtaining infallible evidence on the matter. It must be granted, hence, that we cannot know beyond all question that any given act a person does actually fulfils the criteria of our moral injunction. Must we therefore admit that moral knowledge is not possible? I think not. For there is one person who can know what the reason for doing an act is—the agent himself. Unlike outsiders, he has direct access to his own thoughts and motivations. Even though no one else can assert beyond any shadow of a doubt what his reason for doing an act is, he can. Therefore, he is in a position to judge that, because the act has negative moral effects and because his reason for doing it is equally a reason for not doing it, it is an act that he ought not to do. And this he can know.

But an objection might be raised here. As Kant has emphasized, not even the agent can know what his *real* reason in doing any action is. When it comes to a question of what motivations actually precipitate our actions, we can be as much fooled ourselves as we can fool others. Although Kant may be correct here, I do not think his point touches my case. For even if we were to grant that an agent is mistaken about his real reason for doing an act, we could still maintain that he *knows* what reason *he thinks to be* his real reason for doing it. And that is all that matters. If a person, mistakenly or not, believes that he is doing an act for a certain reason, then, if this reason satisfies the criteria of our moral injunction, the act is one he ought not to do.

The problem of knowledge could be raised concerning one other point in the moral injunction. I have said that an act, to be subject to moral judgment, must have negative moral effects. But how is it possible for us ever to know that an act does have negative moral effects? Can we ever say with certainty that the performance of a certain act will decrease the happiness, hinder the welfare, or run counter to the interests of anyone? I think the same kind of answer can be given to this objection as to the last. Even though no one may know that performance of an act will actually decrease anyone's happiness, he can think that it will, and can know that he thinks this. Thus, a person who performs an act believing that it will decrease the happiness of another and does it for a reason that is equally a reason for not doing it has acted immorally and can know that he has done so.

7. THE PRINCIPLE OF PERSONAL IMPARTIALITY

I have spent a good bit of time defending my contention that the French military commander's act in executing his men was immoral. Yet, it might well be asked, to what purpose have I done this? For even if I have succeeded in making my case, it could be argued that I have not really gained much. Technically, of course, I shall have succeeded in refuting the moral skeptics, but the victory will be only an academic one, for the example of an item of moral knowledge I have found is so esoteric and detached from the lives of most people and the moral decisions they have to make as to be all but irrelevant to any meaningful consideration of the problem of morality, as an issue of vital human interest.

This criticism is, I think, a reasonable one and merits an answer. To provide an answer to it will be one of my main objectives in the remainder of the book. What I shall attempt to show is that my moral injunction can be applied, not just to extreme examples like the one I have given, but to the practical decisions of everyday life. To begin my argument I shall return to the case of the French commander to try to generalize from it a rule of moral action that can be applied in other situations.[1]

If we were asked to state, in general terms, why the commander's act was immoral, I think we should say that the reason lay in its essential arbitrariness. He had no more reason to execute any one-tenth of his men than any other one-tenth. Because the act was essentially arbitrary, he could give no reason to justify it. So we might restate our moral injunction to read "One ought never arbitrarily to do any act that has negative moral effects." Given this general injunction what we must now do in order to make it applicable to concrete moral situations is to formulate some specific criterion in terms of which we can judge the arbitrariness of an act. We already know from our original formulation of the injunction that an arbitrary act is one done for a reason which is logically incapable of justifying it. What we need, therefore, is some principle applicable to the affairs of everyday life that can readily be used to distinguish, among the reasons given for doing acts, between those reasons which can justify

---

[1] It should be noted that I do not rest my case on this particular example or on *any* example, for that matter, but rather on logical considerations. The illustrations I use serve the purpose simply of helping to make clear what these logical considerations are and how they can be applied to practical affairs. I would agree with Kant that principles of morality cannot be derived from examples.

the acts in question and those which cannot. Here again our example can help us. The reason why the commander's act was arbitrary lay in the fact that the men selected for execution differed from their fellows *only* in that they happened to be standing at the fatal spots in the line. The difference between them and their fellows was nothing more than a numerical one. Thus the commander, basing his choice on numerical considerations alone, could with equal justice—or, really, injustice—have selected any other tenth of his men for execution. Every single individual within his command satisfied the numerical conditions for inclusion in some ten per cent of the total, hence could on that basis have been chosen for execution. Therefore, the men actually selected possessed no characteristics used as a basis for selection not equally possessed by every other man in the command. It was for this reason that the commander's act was arbitrary.

Generalizing the argument we can conclude that no individual's numerical uniqueness from his fellows can ever justify our acting toward him in a morally discriminatory way. Because numerical uniqueness is an attribute that every individual possesses equally, the attempt to justify treating a person in a morally discriminatory way on the basis of his numerical uniqueness alone is to imply a justification for treating every other person in the same discriminatory way. But if everyone is treated in the same way, the action is no longer discriminatory. Thus the reason given for such discriminatory treatment is equally a reason for non-discriminatory treatment. So this reason cannot be used—and the "cannot" here expresses a logical impossibility—to justify discriminating in our actions among persons. We have now a principle of moral action that is potentially applicable to the concrete, practical decisions of everyday life. I shall call it the Principle of Personal Impartiality and formulate it as follows: One ought never to do an act having negative moral effects that discriminates between people on the basis of their numerical uniqueness alone.

My principle of personal impartiality, as I have just stated it, looks a good bit like a famous moral slogan, the classical utilitarians' "Everyone to count for one and no one to count for more than one." So it might be asked just how close my theory comes to utilitarianism on this point. The answer depends on what precisely the utilitarians meant by their slogan. If it implies a strict egalitarianism, as it has sometimes been interpreted to do, then my view does not necessarily coincide with it. For all that my principle implies is that discrimination between people on the basis of their numerical uniqueness *alone* is morally unjustifiable. It does not hold that there are no other justifiable grounds for discrimination. What I should argue is that, if such discrimination is to be morally defended, then other reasons must be given for it than the numerical uniqueness of the people concerned. One of my tasks (which I shall take up more fully in the next chapter) will be to decide whether such discrimination ever can be justified and, if so, under what conditions and for what reasons.

Before ending this section I should like to consider an objection that might be raised against my theory, to the effect that my principle that one ought never to discriminate between persons on the basis of their numerical uniqueness alone is too sweeping. For it would condemn activities that many of us believe to be morally legitimate, including, for example, any use of choice by lot. Should we censure the ancient Athenians who awarded political positions to their citizens by lot? Or the people who run the Irish sweepstakes? Discrimination by lot is analogous, it would seem, to the kind of action I have condemned in that in both the principle of selection is arbitrary. The only reason why John Doe (rather than some other one of the millions of ticket holders) wins a fortune in the sweepstakes is that he is holding the number drawn. It is his numerical uniqueness alone, *vis à vis* this lottery, that marks him out for special favor. Nevertheless, I believe that the analogy on which the objection rests breaks down. For it is possible to distinguish between arbitrary discrimination that is morally acceptable and that is not. The difference between the two is in the position of those who are, either actually or potentially, discriminated against. In my illustration from the war the victims were arbitrarily executed against their will. The commander never secured the prior approval of his troops to employ this kind of tactic to achieve his ends. Had he actually done so, I think the situation would have been altered morally. For then, even though he still could not have justified rationally his choices for execution, it could be argued that he would not have had to do so. (I would not want to say flatly that in this situation such consent would exonerate the commander for that would imply that an act's satisfaction of the conditions of my moral injunction provides a necessary condition for our judging the act to be immoral and I am not sure that this is true.)

To return to the illustrations just cited, the Athenian constitution provided for choice by lot and the citizens presumably were in favor of such a system even though it meant that many suffered from arbitrary discrimination at election time. And those who do not win in the sweepstakes presumably are more than willing to accept the probable eventuality that they will be victims of arbitrary discrimination when they buy their tickets, on the small chance that the discrimination may turn out to be in their favor. It is this prior approval of the arbitrary discriminatory act by those directly affected that marks the difference between arbitrary action that may very well be morally acceptable and action that I have contended to be morally reprehensible. The same point could be made in another way, by saying that the acts in question, in the case of formalized selection by lot, do not have "negative moral effects" (see above, § 4).

8. EGOISM AND MORALITY

My principle of personal impartiality is clearly and directly incompatible with one view regarding the moral relationships between human beings that has had many defenders among professional philosophers and laymen alike. This is egoism. If it be true, as I have maintained in my principle of personal impartiality, that one ought never to perform an action having negative moral effects that discriminates between persons on the basis of their numerical uniqueness alone, it would seem to follow that it cannot be true that anyone can be morally justified in seeking his own welfare exclusively, without regard to the interests of others.[1] The conflict between my position and egoism is particularly important for the problem of moral knowledge because, if egoism is true, it follows that no one has any moral obligations. For the egoist, when he says that everyone "ought" to seek his own welfare exclusively, is not laying down a moral injunction but rather denying all moral injunctions. The "ought" in his statement is not the moral, but the prudential "ought." What he is implying is that it is a mistake to believe that there is a distinctive moral dimension to human life and personal relationships. Therefore, if we think clearly and act accordingly, we will devote all of our efforts to securing our own personal welfare without regard to that of anyone else.

[1] I shall limit my discussion here to what may be called extreme egoism, the view that each individual ought to seek his own welfare exclusively, without any regard to the welfare of others, rather than moderate egoism, which holds that each individual should always give precedence to his own welfare over that of others yet at the same time acknowledges that there are situations in which an individual can rightly be said to have duties to others. Although both types of egoism are incompatible with my principle of personal impartiality, only the extreme egoistic position, by denying the existence of moral obligation altogether, implies the impossibility of moral knowledge. Hence, I must refute it if I am to defend my thesis that we have duties and can know that we do.

The incompatibility between egoism and my principle of personal impartiality is quite apparent. Because the egoist advocates the performance of acts having negative moral effects that discriminate between persons on the basis of their numerical uniqueness alone, he directly rejects my principle. Hence, if the principle be granted to be demonstrably true, it follows that an egoistic course of action is equally demonstrably immoral. Because egoistic action cannot be morally justified, egoism must be rejected as false, so cannot provide a basis from which to deny the reality of moral obligation and, by implication, the possibility of moral knowledge.

This conclusion is, however, open to question, on the grounds that egoistic action does not really violate my principle of personal impartiality. For the person who seeks his own welfare exclusively does not, as I assume he does, single himself out for preferential treatment on the basis of his numerical uniqueness alone. Although it may well be true that a person who had discriminated in an action affecting two other people, A and B, on the grounds simply that A was A and B was B could be legitimately accused of having violated my principle, the situation is different when one of the two people affected by the act is the agent himself. For the agent, as the beneficiary of his own action, can always be distinguished from all other possible beneficiaries of that action in one way that is not reducible simply to numerical difference. As beneficiary of the act he bears a relationship to the agent that no other beneficiary possibly can—the relationship of identity. If asked to justify his action morally, even if he has no other reason to give, he can always say "I did it to promote *my own* greatest welfare." And this reason neither rests on an appeal to his numerical uniqueness alone nor is a reason that would be equally a reason for his doing another act instead, because no other person stands in the same relationship to the person himself, as agent.

If we assume, with the objector, that egoistic action does not violate my principle of personal impartiality because the principle does not apply to it, we seem to be left with no argument capable of refuting egoism, and its implied a-moralism. However, it does not necessarily follow from this that no one has any moral obligations whatsoever, because the egoistic argument applies only to situations in which the person being helped by the action contemplated is the agent himself. In situations (of which the French commander's is an example) in which the decision concerns a choice between individuals or groups of individuals other than the agent, the argument would not apply and my principle of personal impartiality would still hold good. Hence in all such situations we could maintain that the agent has a moral obligation to act impartially.

But I think that the argument against the egoists can be pressed further. We may grant their contention that every individual, as an agent, stands in a unique relationship to himself as beneficiary of his own action but deny that the uniqueness of this relationship is relevant to the issue under consideration. The central operative concept in my principle of personal impartiality is the notion of "numerical uniqueness." In what respect does the principle hold that the numerical uniqueness of a person cannot justify discriminatory treatment? Or, what kind of numerical uniqueness is the principle concerned with when it denies that numerical uniqueness can justify discrimination? The answer is—the numerical uniqueness of a person *insofar as* he is a person affected by the action (but not insofar as he is a person related in any way to the agent). The distinction I am trying to make here is a difficult one to state but it is crucial. What I am saying is that, according to the principle of personal impartiality, one ought never (because it is rationally indefensible) to discriminate between people who will be affected by any act he might do solely on the basis of their numerical uniqueness, considering the numerical uniqueness of each in respect of him simply as a possible beneficiary of the act. Now the argument for egoism that I have presented succeeds in establishing only that each individual, as such, is unique, in the relationship between himself as agent and as the beneficiary of action, in a way different from simple numerical uniqueness. It does not establish that each individual, as such, has any uniqueness, considered as a beneficiary of action, that goes beyond numerical uniqueness, no matter who the agent acting might be. And it is the second thesis that must be established to exempt egoistic action from moral judgment under my principle of personal impartiality.[1]

9. THE DEDUCTIVE FALLACY

Before concluding this chapter, I should like to discuss one crucial question concerning the theory I have been presenting: Does it succeed in avoiding the deductive fallacy? Let us imagine a person considering the performance of some act and trying to decide whether, according

---

[1] There is one other argument that an egoist could use to avoid moral censure under my principle. I shall discuss it in the next chapter (8.1).

to my theory, he would be justified in doing it. He might argue in the following way:

Act X (the act contemplated) has negative moral effects

My reason for doing act X is equally a reason for not doing it

Therefore, I ought not to do act X.

As it stands, this argument is clearly fallacious. Since the premises do not contain an "ought" but the conclusion does, it cannot be logically derived from them and we have an obvious case of the deductive fallacy. Fortunately, the difficulty can be easily overcome. All that is needed is the insertion into the argument of my moral injunction as a new major premise. The argument would now read:

One ought never to do an act having negative moral effects if his reason for doing the act is equally a reason for not doing it

Act X has negative moral effects and my reason for doing it is equally a reason for not doing it

Therefore, I ought not to do act X.

This argument does not commit the deductive fallacy in the way in which the first one does for it is clearly cogent logically. Assuming that the premises are true, it follows that the conclusion is true as well. Therefore, I could know that I ought not to do act X.

But my conclusion here must be examined further. Even though my second argument succeeds in avoiding the more obvious horn of the deductive fallacy, does it not become impaled on the less obvious one? My whole case rests on the assumption that the premises of my argument can be known to be true. The critical one is the major premise, which contains my moral injunction. I have contended that this premise is self-evidently true. However, it might be argued against me that it is really question-begging. The reason why I say that one ought never to do an act having negative moral effects if his reason for doing the act is equally a reason for not doing it is that performance of such an act is rationally indefensible. Therefore, to justify my moral injunction I must assume that one ought never to act arbitrarily (*i.e.*, without reason). My argument could be stated formally in this way:

One ought never to act arbitrarily if one's act has negative moral effects

To do an act having negative moral effects for which the reason given is equally a reason for not doing the act is to act arbitrarily

Therefore, one ought never to do an act having negative moral effects if his reason for doing the act is equally a reason for not doing it.

The criticism of my theory could be formulated as follows: My argument is question-begging because it rests on the assumption, appearing in the major premise of the syllogism, that one ought never to act arbitrarily (if the act has negative moral effects). But, if one rejects this assumption, then the conclusion (my moral injunction) collapses. Or, put in the other way, my moral injunction holds good only if the assumption that one ought never to act arbitrarily is accepted. But why accept this assumption? How can it be defended?

The answer I must give to these questions is that the assumption is logically self-evident because its denial involves a contradiction. Anyone who denies it must hold that it is morally justifiable to perform an arbitrary act having negative moral effects. Such a position, I would argue, is logically indefensible, for two reasons: (1) Morality is concerned with the reasons we give for what we do. As I explained in § 3, the notion of moral obligation derives its meaning from the circumstances of man's relationships with his fellows. Morality is man's attempt to adjudicate the conflicts between himself and others rationally. When a person contemplates performing an act and discovers that doing it will harm someone else, if he responds morally, he will do the act only if he can justify performing it. Before acting he will find some good reason for what he does. And if he finds no good reason yet goes ahead anyaway, then his act is immoral. (2) An arbitrary act is an act done without reason. But an act done without reason cannot be an act done with good reason. Therefore, since an act having negative moral effects must, to be morally defensible, be one done with a good reason, an arbitrary act is morally indefensible—an act that one ought not to do.

But is this answer complete? Might a critic not argue that I have succeeded only in pushing the problem one step back? For my conclusion that we ought not to act arbitrarily because morality demands that we justify our actions rests on the general assumption that we *ought* to base our beliefs about what we ought to do on reason. But how can the "ought" that I have just italicized be justified? Are we not committed here to an infinite regress and hence caught by the deductive fallacy? Let us look at the situation more closely in order to define the issue precisely. My position is (1) that an act, to be moral, must be justified and (2) that no act done without reason can be justified therefore (3) that an arbitrary act must be immoral. Now, the criticism runs, my conclusion is coercive only to someone who accepts the appeal to reason as a criterion of truth. But it cannot touch the irrationalist, who is unmoved by argument. To conclude that I have established my case because I have demonstrated it rationally is to beg the question against him.

I would agree that my conclusion cannot coerce anyone who is unmoved by argument but I would deny that it begs any question therefore requires an infinite regress to substantiate itself. As I argued early in the chapter (§ 2), a question can be begged only if there is a question to be begged. This implies that the person opposing me must have a position which my argument illegitimately slights. But the irrationalist has no such position. He can *say* "I refuse to be influenced by reason" and no one can touch him but he cannot defend this stand in any way whatsoever because to do so he would have to appeal to the very reason he is rejecting, hence abandon his irrationalism. As a matter of fact, if he asks "Why ought one to be rational?" and expects me to answer him, he is begging the question against me because he is demanding that I give him reasons to support my view and he has already taken the stand that no reasons will have any effect on him. The irrationalist's stand, because it is intrinsically indefensible, can be legitimately disregarded. Its interest is only psychological, not theoretical. To put my argument in another way, the "assumption" that a theory, to merit consideration (or even to qualify as a theory for that matter), must operate within the domain of rationality and accept its canons is not really an assumption at all, because it cannot be denied. Therefore, a moral skeptic who tries to base his skepticism on a complete rejection of reason would have no case. Indeed, he could not even state his position without by that very act giving it up. My answer to him, thus, would win a conclusive victory by default. So I have aimed my argument at the reasonable skeptic, who attempts to base his conclusions on reason and who is willing to accept what is demonstrated to him, because he is the only one who has a case that I must answer. And I have already given my reasons for concluding that my justification of moral obligation does succeed in answering him.

CHAPTER VIII

TOWARD A GENERAL THEORY OF MORALITY

What I should like to do in this last chapter is to give a brief, and quite cursory sketch of a general theory of morality, based on the conclusions that I reached in Chapter VII. In addition, I should like to discuss further a few scattered points that I raised at various times earlier in the book, but did not then treat fully. The argument of the chapter, consequently, will be diffuse rather than precise and general rather than detailed. My object will be served, however, if I am able to indicate the main lines that I believe a satisfactory theory of the moral life must follow. To develop such a theory from the conclusions I reached in the last chapter. I shall attempt to do the following: (1) Derive a positive theory of moral obligation from the negative one I have already elaborated and (2) justify certain practical qualifications in the extreme position on moral obligation that my theory seems to imply. I shall take up these two tasks first.

1. OUTLINE OF A POSITIVE THEORY OF OBLIGATION

The reader has probably noted that the moral injunction that I elaborated in the last chapter, "One ought never to do an act having negative moral effects if his reason for doing the act is equally a reason for not doing it," is stated *negatively*. It tells us what we ought not to do but not what we ought to do. So the question naturally arises, Can this negative formulation be transformed into a positive one? Actually, the ingredients for such a transformation have already been given. In explaining the moral injunction in the last chapter (7.4), I pointed out that the term "negative moral effects," besides meaning consequences that affect people other than the agent adversely, means as well consequences that affect a limited number of people, which may include the agent, favorably. Such consequences, if considered from the point of view of the people who do not share in them, are negative because they discriminate against them. Following out this point, I argued that it is immoral to perform such an act, if one has no good reason to give for doing it. Thus, we obtain from this interpretation of the notion of "negative moral effects" a moral injunction against acts that arbitrarily discriminate against individuals by promoting without reason the happiness of some at the expense of others. In the last chapter I argued as well (7.3) that moral problems arise out of the conflicts of human interests. I should like to develop this point somewhat further, because I believe that it, in conjunction with the interpretation of "negative moral effects" that I have just discussed, can provide a basis for the statement of a positive moral injunction.

According to Aristotle, all men seek "happiness." The English word, happiness, is particularly felicitous—as long as one avoids the hedonists' error of identifying happiness with pleasure—mainly because it is so vague. One can without undue straining of the language include within its meaning all of the manifold and diverse strivings of men, from the alcoholic's pursuit of a happy state of oblivion through intoxication to the mystic's search for happiness in union with the divine. To say that we all seek happiness, however, is not necessarily to imply that we are psychological egoists. That would be true only if we sought nothing but our own happiness. I do not think it is necessary any longer to spend time on a refutation of psychological egoism. Suffice it to say that it is evident that all of us do devote some of our energies to promoting the happiness of others. Nevertheless, if we were to state in a general way the primary goal of each individual's strivings, I think we could reasonably agree with Aristotle in saying that it is his own happiness. And it is this search that leads to the problems of morality, which stem from the inevitable conflicts that arise when one individual's pursuit of happiness interferes with that of another.

One of the main conclusions of the last chapter was that it is immoral for an individual to further his own happiness, or that of any limited group of people, at the expense of the rest just because it is his own happiness. But, if we accept the fact that it is natural for all of us to seek happiness, we seem to be caught in a dilemma between our strivings, as beings of will and desire, on the one hand, and our recognition, as beings of reason, on the other, of an opposing moral injunction. We can overcome this apparent opposition by recognizing that we can justify morally the pursuit of our own happiness on one condition—that we promote the happiness of all others equally with our own. Assuming, then, both the universality of the human quest for happiness and the necessity for providing a moral justification for that quest, we can lay down the positive moral injunction: "One ought always to promote impartially the happiness of all people" or "Everyone has a duty to promote the happiness of all individuals equally." If a person fulfils this obligation, then he can, with a clear conscience, seek the personal happiness he desires.

This positive statement of the moral injunction, it may be noted, is extreme. By making our duties extend to all people equally, it eliminates any reference to time or place, implying that we owe as much morally to the most remote inhabitants of the interior of China as we do to the members of our own community and as much to our possible ancestors a thousand years hence as to our contemporaries. Unless we can justify some limitation on the scope of our obligation, as rational beings we must accept this universal duty.

One theoretical limitation can, I think, be made immediately. We do not have a duty to do the impossible. If I cannot perform an act, then, even if it is an act that falls under the moral injunction, I am relieved of my obligation to do it. Thus, I have no duty to promote the welfare of Southern slaves; I am living a hundred years too late. Nor am I obligated to eliminate suffering from the world; I cannot do it. Nevertheless, I do have an obligation to mitigate suffering because this I can to some extent do. The use of the argument that "ought" implies "can" to limit our duties is, I believe, just—as long as we remain in the realm of theory. But when we turn to practical life problems suddenly descend on us. For who can with confidence draw the line between the possible and the impossible? Sometimes the line seems fairly clear, as in a situation in which fulfilment of an obligation would require the reversal of time. But generally there is little clarity; one simply does not know what he can and cannot do. Does any medical scientist have an obligation to find a cure for cancer? Did anyone have a duty to find a method for preventing poliomyelitis? Under what conditions can a person relieve himself of moral responsibility in an automobile accident in which someone else is hurt or killed—because he was intoxicated and could not control his vehicle, because he had failed to repair faulty brakes so was unable to stop, because he had a sudden heart seizure while driving? I shall not attempt to answer these practical questions here; however in the next section I shall return to the subject of possible limitations on the universality of my positive moral injunction.

In the meanwhile I shall take up once more the subject of moral egoism, to consider an argument that the egoists might use against me,

which I did not raise in my discussion of egoism in the last chapter
(7.8). My argument there assumed that egoism, as a theory of moral
action, is incompatible with my principle of personal impartiality. But
an egoist might defend himself, not by the argument (which I attempted to refute in 7.8) that my principle does not apply to actions whose
beneficiary is the agent himself, but by the contention that egoistic
action is not really incompatible with my principle. To make his case,
the egoist would have to interpret the principle somewhat broadly but
he could maintain that his interpretation does not unduly violate it.
His argument would run along these lines: The principle of personal
impartiality (in its positive form) states that we ought to promote the
happiness of all individuals equally, thus it appears to be incompatible
with egoism, which holds that we are morally free to promote our own
happiness exclusively. However, this apparent incompatibility disappears if we realize that a course of action leading to one's own greatest
welfare will *in the long run* result in the greatest possible welfare of all
other individuals as well. Or, put in the other way, if our aim is to
promote the greatest welfare of all other individuals, then a feasible
method for achieving this goal is to concentrate all of our efforts on
pursuing our own welfare.

I think that this defense of egoism is open to attack on two counts,
one practical and the other theoretical. On the practical side, the
egoists' contention that a policy of strict self-interested action is the
best (or even a reasonable) method for attaining the greatest happiness
of all is highly questionable. I do not see how the contention can be
refuted logically, for the egoists have a built- in answer to all possible
objections, to the effect that, no matter how much the evidence of
experience may appear to be against their view, in the long run the
balance is redressed. Even though a policy of self-interested action may
seem to cause unhappiness to others, this unhappiness is merely tempo-
rary; when the final results of such a policy are considered, it will be
seen that the general happiness produced far outweighs the unhappiness. Since it is impossible to put an end to the consequences that can
be held to be relevant to any course of action, we can never demonstrate conclusively that the egoists' expectations are unwarranted.
Nevertheless, although we may not be able to refute the egoists' case
conclusively, I believe that we have good reasons for rejecting it. For
it is highly implausible, running directly against the great bulk of
human experience. The evidence that we have regarding human
relationships and the effects of an individual's actions on the happiness

of others, considered over a long period of time, does not support at all the view that the most successful way of contributing to the welfare of others is through a deliberate policy of acting without any regard for that welfare. To assume the contrary, as the egoists do, is to imply a radical perversity in the course of nature or an egregious stupidity on the part of humanity, or both.

I turn now to a theoretical criticism of egoism, which is more important, as far as the problem of moral knowledge is concerned, than the practical objection I have just raised. To begin the argument it is necessary to point out a difference between the kind of egoism I discussed in the last chapter (7.8) and the kind I am concerned with here. The former type of position, which could appropriately be called *theoretical* egoism, is a theory about *ends*; it holds that everyone is morally free to seek his own happiness exclusively, as an end in itself, without regard to the happiness of anyone else. In doing so it clearly eliminates the moral "ought" from human life, leaving only the prudential "ought." The egoism I am now considering could be called *pragmatic* egoism; it is an egoism not of ends but of *means*. Rather than justifying egoistic action by the argument that it promotes the welfare of the agent, it justifies such action by the claim that it provides the most efficient means for achieving the greatest possible happiness of all. So the question can be raised, Does pragmatic egoism replace the moral "ought" with the prudential "ought"? Not at all. On the contrary, it implies an acceptance of the moral "ought." For, if one argues that we ought always to act prudentially, on the grounds that prudential action best promotes the general welfare, then he is assuming that we have a duty to promote the general welfare. But this is to accept rather than to reject the moral "ought." What distinguishes the pragmatic egoist from other moralists is not his denial of the existence of moral obligation but his odd, and highly implausible, account of how we can best go about fulfilling our obligations to our fellows. Because it does not reject the moral "ought," pragmatic egoism can provide no basis for an argument denying the possibility of moral knowledge.

2. PRACTICAL QUALIFICATIONS

In the last section I argued that we all have a moral obligation, limited only by the bounds of possibility, to promote impartially the happiness of all people. This is a heavy obligation, one that none of us comes near fulfilling. What I should like to do in this section is to suggest certain limitations in the scope of our duties and then attempt to show that these can be justified without violating the moral injunction itself. Before doing this, however, I think I ought to point out that the positive moral injunction that I have stated, although it lays us all under an extreme obligation, does nevertheless reflect a tradition, both in belief and practice, within our civilization regarding the nature and scope of our duties.

Our Christian tradition offers many examples of a view much like mine. An obvious illustration is the story of the good Samaritan, from the gospel of St. Luke. To appreciate the significance of that story one has to remember that it constituted Jesus' answer to a lawyer, who had asked him concerning the second commandment ("Thou shalt love thy neighbor as thyself"), "But, master, just who is my neighbor?" Jesus' reply, given in the form of the parable of the good Samaritan, was that *anyone*, no matter what his external condition or status might be, is our neighbor and ought to be treated accordingly. Turning to a consideration of actual practice we find numerous illustrations of the fact that people have recognized an obligation to others far removed from them. The recognition given to the rights of future, unborn generations is a case in point. It appears fairly obviously, for example, in our national park system, in which the government has set aside large areas of scenic and naturally beautiful land as parks for places of recreation and enjoyment for centuries to come. It is clear that the early leaders in the national park movement were not thinking simply of the welfare of their own generation or even that of their grandchildren. For the full recreational exploitation of these vast areas of unspoiled nature has not nearly arrived yet and they will, barring unforeseen changes in the history of the world, furnish enjoyment for many generations to come.

However, even though we may ideally accept a universal obligation to our fellow men and even make some attempts to meet this obligation in practice, the fact remains that all of us fall far short of fulfilling it. We are all, thus, morally culpable and must bear the responsibility for our shortcomings. Nevertheless, I think that it is possible to justify, at least to some extent, our failure to satisfy fully the obligation laid down by the moral injunction. For one can make a case for the view that a person can be morally justified in furthering his own happiness and that of those near to him in place and time in preference to that of those widely separated from him. The argument, which involves two main steps, is best understood if we approach the moral situation from the side, not of the agent, but of those affected by his acts. To say that the agent has a moral obligation to consider their happiness is to imply that they have a right to expect him to do so. In fact, they can demand (morally) that he do so. It is their possession of such a right that creates his duty. A duty owed, in other words, implies a right possessed. Therefore, because the agent's duty depends on the possession by the potential beneficiaries of certain rights, these beneficiaries can at their discretion give up these rights and release him from his obligation to them. An act that would normally be his duty in such a situation is no longer obligatory on him.

Now I would argue that all of us do release others from their normal obligations to us and that we have what we believe to be a good reason for doing so. Our reason for demanding fulfilment of these obligations is a prudential one; we wish others to contribute to our happiness just as they wish us to contribute to theirs. So it is natural for us, in situations in which the insistence on our rights will result in a smaller increase in our happiness than the waiver of these rights would do, to release others from their obligations to us. Such situations occur constantly because we recognize that the happiness of all—and, consequently, our own happiness—can be most efficiently promoted by a social arrangement in which each individual fulfils his obligations most fully to (or makes the most consistent direct contribution to the happiness of) a small circle of people nearest to him, less fully to a wider circle of friends and acquaintances, only occasionally to his community as a whole, and rarely or never to society at large. Experience has proved such a practical limitation on the scope of our activities on behalf of the happiness of others to be justified by its results. For each of us can realize a greater happiness under such an arrangement than would be possible in a situation in which everyone attempted to fulfil his whole obligation to all other people completely. So we consent to releasing others from their obligations to us on the assumption that they will do the same for us.

The second step of the argument consists in broadening the notion of consent, to provide a justification for discrimination as a general practice. What people as a matter of fact do is assume that those who have not actually released us from our moral obligations to them, perhaps because they live far away or have not yet been born, would do so if they were asked, because they would recognize that their doing so would, for the kind of reasons given in the last paragraph, result in greater happiness for them than would their refusal to do so. We assume, in other words, their *tacit* consent, releasing us from our obligations to them. It seems to me that such an assumption can be practically justified. Would it be reasonable for me, for example, to be as concerned about providing for the financial security of my great-great grandchildren as for that of my own children? It seems to me not. For the chances of my being able to accomplish anything toward that end with any degree of efficiency are slender indeed. For the greatest financial security of all concerned, it would be far better for me to leave that of their children to my great grandchildren and concentrate my attention on the welfare of my own children. And I think that I am reasonably justified in assuming that, if they were alive now, these great-great grandchildren would agree with me and release me from any financial obligation to them.

It is obvious that the kind of reasoning I have just been defending presents serious dangers. For we are too apt to assume that others tacitly consent to our discriminatory practices in situations in which there are no adequate reasons why they should give such consent. On the whole, we are prone too readily to assume that we need not concern ourselves about the happiness of those with whom we are not directly associated. We quite overlook the needs and aspirations of the people of Asia or Africa or the welfare of future generations to concentrate our attention on the interests of our own country and our own generation. Often such a restriction of interest is the result of motivations that are morally indefensible. We simply have no concern for the welfare of anyone but ourselves and contribute to that of others only to the extent that the pressures of society force us to do so. Sometimes, however, we fall short for a quite different reason. Like those who preceded the good Samaritan down the road past the suffering traveller, although we may be aware of the moral claims of those near to us, we do not recognize the needs of strangers and people separated from us. What we lack more than anything else is imagination—the ability to dissociate ourselves from our own particular context and look at the world through the eyes of others, even those quite different from ourselves. Although the gift of imagination is probably not equally distributed, I think that almost all of us could enlarge our own capacities if we paused and took the time before we acted to consider seriously and reflectively the full consequences of what we were about to do.

My aim in this and the preceding section has been to sketch the outlines of a positive theory of moral obligation, applicable not just to extraordinary situations (like that of the French commander) but to the everyday decisions of ordinary life. I should emphasize that my statement is only an outline; it presents simply the general criteria in terms of which we can make our moral decisions and defend those decisions once they have been made. I have not attempted to go into the details of practical morality, since these do not fall within the scope of the present book. I need hardly say that the problems involved in trying to apply the criteria of moral action that I have given to the practical moral situations we have to face are enormous and that it is, consequently, very difficult for a person who has to make a moral decision ever to know if he has decided correctly. But then, no moral theory worthy of serious consideration can provide us with a simple and unequivocal solution to the individual practical problems that arise each day. What a theory can, and practically should do is to provide some criterion or set of criteria that we can use as a general guide in seeking solutions to these problems. This, I believe, the theory I have presented does do. And by doing so it gives us an alternative to moral skepticism. The conclusion we found ourselves forced to after a review of the major contemporary theories of moral obligation was that any satisfactory theory, in order to escape the deductive fallacy, must be based on a self-evident moral proposition. In order not to succumb to the charge of begging the question (as the intuitionists do), we found it necessary to seek a proposition asserting a moral obligation that was logically self-evident. This was my moral injunction "One ought never to do an act having negative moral effects if his reason for doing the act is equally a reason for not doing it" (which I formulated in 7.4). The remainder of my case has been developed from this original injunction. If I may comment on my own theory, I should say that it seems to me clear that the general method I have used (the appeal to a logically self-evident moral axiom) provides the only defensible alternative to moral skepticism and that it is a real, viable alternative. I think, too, that the moral injunction that I have given, whether it be stated in this or some roughly equivalent way, must form the foundation for any theory of moral obligation that can be defended against the attacks of the skeptics. As for the further articulation of my theory, in this and the preceding chapter, although I would be prepared to defend each major step in my argument, I am inclined to believe that there are other routes by which the theory could be developed and that development following a somewhat different path than mine might well be more successful in communicating the view that I have been trying to present.

3. MORALITY AND UTILITY

Someone reading the argument of the last two chapters might well be led to observe that the main conclusions about the moral life that I have reached, rather than being novel, bear a remarkable resemblance to the views of the classical utilitarians. For their two slogans, "the greatest happiness of the greatest number" and "everyone to count for one and no one to count for more than one," typify an ideal of moral action that seems little different from the one that I have presented here. Such an observation would, I think, be just; however I would not take it as a criticism of what I have done. For I would agree, in general, with the classical utilitarians' theory of morality—although I would reject their identification of happiness with pleasure, considering my conclusions more consonant with *ideal* than with *hedonistic* utilitarianism. For me the important question in this book has not been, Are the utilitarians' views about how we ought to act correct? but rather, Are the arguments by which they support these views cogent? and, in particular, Do these arguments succeed in providing good reasons for the belief that we have a moral obligation to act in the way that the utilitarians (or anyone else for that matter) say we do? Now I have contended that the theories of most moral philosophers, including the utilitarians, cannot answer these last questions satisfactorily, because their attempts to provide a theoretical justification of moral obligation all commit the deductive fallacy. My object in this book has not been to elaborate a novel view of human morality but rather to find an argument which will be capable of providing support for some view, whether it be old or new. I think that a theory of the moral life that is broadly utilitarian in nature can be defended against the moral skeptics and that the argument I have outlined in the last chapter and the first two sections of this chapter gives the logical defense of it that it has until the present lacked. To provide this logical defense I have abandoned traditional ways of solving the problem of moral knowledge, to deal with the issue by a quite different method. It is in my methodological departure from tradition in coping with the problem of moral knowledge that I would hope that the main novelty of my theory lies.

Some moral philosophers would object to the utilitarian conclusions I seem to be accepting on the grounds that, although many of our duties can be accounted for by some form of utilitarian explanation, others fall outside the scope of any view, no matter how argued, which bases morality on the consequences of our actions, hence no form of utilitarianism can ever furnish us with a complete theory of the moral life. Such a criticism would come, for example, from deontologists like Prichard and Ross (see 2.2). The objections these writers make against utilitarianism are, I believe, serious and demand careful consideration. To do them justice not only would require much more space than I have here but would lead into problems quite distinct from that of moral knowledge, which has been my concern in this book. Since I have discussed the deontologists' case against ideal utilitarianism at length elsewhere, I shall not take up the subject further now.[1] Suffice it to say that I think the theory I have presented here can avoid the objections they raise against utilitarianism.

4. GOODNESS AND THE NATURALISTIC FALLACY

The theory of morality that I have proposed is based on two charac-teristics of man, his desires or inclinations, whose object is happiness, and his reason. All of us desire happiness but in our search for that goal we find ourselves in conflict with each other. If we were animals we would resolve such conflicts by brute strength or by cunning. But, because we are capable of reason, we can examine our actions critically and recognize that we do not have good reasons to give for many of the things that we want to do. Thus we become moral beings, able to decide how we ought to act. (Whether we succeed in putting our decisions into practice is, of course, quite another question, which takes us out of the realm of moral philosophy altogether into that of practical morality.)

It might be noted that there is an important omission in the theory of morality which I have outlined; nowhere in it do I make any reference to the concepts of good and evil. Since these notions have been considered fundamental to moral theory by most philosophers

---

[1] In my *Rightness and Goodness*. Although I would not now accept either the concept-ual framework in which my argument in that book is cast nor the appeal to moral insight on which many of my main conclusions rest, I still believe that the "axiological" position that I defend in it (which is an expanded form of ideal utilitarianism) provides a more satisfactory account of the moral life than the alternative view offered by the deontologists.

since Plato, the fact that I omit them reveals a basic difference between my approach to moral philosophy and, in particular, to the problem of moral knowledge and that of most traditional writers. I have three main reasons for leaving these notions out of my theory.[1] In the first place, I do not believe that the universe contains any such entities or attributes as good and evil. I shall not argue for this thesis here (since it would require an extremely long digression) but will content myself with a few brief remarks.

It should be clear from what I have already said that I am not, by my denial of the reality of good and evil, supporting any kind of cynicism which would eradicate all moral distinctions and deny that anyone who, in normal talk, uses the words "good" and "evil" is referring to anything meaningful or important. Quite the contrary. The point I am making is strictly a theoretical one; I believe that those philosophers who attempt to base an explanation of morality on the assumption that these concepts do refer to something real run into insuperable difficulties. Perhaps the best illustration is given by G. E. Moore. Probably more than anyone else (with the exception of Plato) Moore was convinced of the reality of goodness, as a quality characterizing especially certain human experiences. He devoted much of his life to an attempt to explain just what kind of characteristic goodness is. Nonetheless, his explanations, brilliant, subtle, and penetrating as they are, fail to be convincing. He began by maintaining—what seems to be apparent from the way in which we normally use the word "good"—that goodness is a quality that characterizes certain things. But just what kind of quality is it? Before he was through answering this question Moore found himself forced to affirm that goodness is a quality that is indefinable, non-natural, intrinsic to whatever possesses it without being an intrinsic quality of what possesses it, non-descriptive, and non-existent. I, for one, am convinced that the world contains no such quality as Moore's "goodness." Moore might, I think, reply to me by arguing that, however implausible it may appear to say that there is a quality of the kind he takes goodness to be, there are overwhelming theoretical reasons forcing us to accept its reality. Specifically, he would continue, acceptance of the reality of goodness provides the only basis on which we can avoid moral skepticism. For, in order to justify our convictions about what we ought to do, we must appeal to the goodness of the consequences of our acts. Now I have

---

[1] I have omitted from the theory the concepts of rightness and wrongness, as attributes of our actions, as well, for the same reasons that I give for omitting good and evil.

argued in Chapter II—and this is my second reason for eliminating goodness from my theory—that Moore is mistaken on this point. Not only is it not true that the appeal to goodness alone will justify our beliefs about our duties but such an appeal is logically unable to support these beliefs at all. For any attempt to use it in their support commits the deductive fallacy.

Finally, it is possible to provide a theoretical justification for morality without appealing to the concept of goodness at all. This is what I have been doing in these last chapters. The appeal to goodness not only can provide no support for our convictions about what we ought to do but is not needed for such support. For we can justify those convictions in quite another way. My theory, containing no reference to goodness at all, does not lead to moral skepticism; on the contrary, I would argue, it provides the only kind of approach to the problem of moral knowledge that can successfully meet the attacks of the skeptics.

Turning from Moore to his main opponents, the naturalists, I should like to comment on a remark I made early in the book. In Chapter II (2.8) I said that, although the naturalists cannot on their assumptions provide any justification for moral obligation, their views can form a part of a theory of the moral life. In the last two chapters I have actually been defending that remark for the theory that I have proposed is, in part, naturalistic. Its naturalism lies in its acceptance of human desires and inclinations simply as facts and its unwillingness to judge these in terms of some external "non-naturalistic" standard of value. It is thus implied by my theory that no answer can be given to a question like "Is such and such a desire good (or bad)?" This implication raises the possibility that the theory might be guilty of the naturalistic fallacy. Now Moore would contend that naturalists (and anyone who attempts to define "good") commit the naturalistic fallacy because, no matter how they define "good," it is always meaningful to ask of anything that satisfies the definition given, "But is it *really* good?" hence that all such definitions are necessarily fallacious. Furthermore, he would argue, the question, Is it good? can be significantly asked of *anything*. Since I have ruled out the possibility of asking of any desire which a person has, Is his desire really good? I seem, like the naturalists, to be running afoul of the naturalistic fallacy.

The standard answer given to Moore by naturalists is that his contention that all definitions of "good" involve a fallacy is question-begging. To justify his thesis that the question "Is so and so (what satisfies a given naturalistic definition of 'good') really good?" is meaningful, they argue, Moore must assume that "good" has a meaning distinct from that in terms of which the naturalist has defined it. But this is exactly what the naturalist is denying. Hence, for Moore to assume the point is to beg the question at issue. I think that the naturalists' reply to Moore is correct, but I do not believe that it overcomes the basic weakness of naturalism. For naturalism is vitiated not by the fact that it attempts to define an indefinable term but rather that it is impossible, from its assumptions, to derive any theory of moral action. This impossibility stems from the fact that any attempt to do so, although it may not commit a "naturalistic fallacy," does commit the deductive fallacy.

But where naturalism fails Moore's intuitionism fails also. One cannot overcome the basic defect of traditional naturalistic ethics by assuming the existence of an intuitively apprehended indefinable quality, goodness. For, as we found in Chapter II, the gap between what is good and the acts that we ought to do is one that no logic can bridge. As far as providing a theory of the moral life is concerned, Moore is finally no more successful than his naturalistic opponents.

It is my belief that, if a form of naturalism is combined with a quite different justification of moral obligation, one based on reason, the result can be a theory of the moral life that is defensible against skeptical attack. In my theory I have attempted to effect such a combination. In the first place, I accept a naturalistic view of man as a being of desires and inclinations, avoiding the "naturalistic fallacy" altogether by maintaining that my naturalistic analysis cannot involve a fallacious definition of "good" simply because there is no concept "goodness" to be defined. But, secondly—and this is the crucial point of difference in my theory—I add a new dimension, that appears neither in the naturalists nor in Moore. This is a justification of moral obligation through reason. For reason tells us directly, without any need of a deductive argument of the kind used both by Moore and the traditional naturalists, what we ought and ought not to do. Thus, a justification of moral obligation can be given which neither involves commission of the deductive fallacy, on the one hand, nor is question-begging, on the other.

According to the theory I have proposed, true ascriptions of obligation do not require a deductive argument or an appeal to intuition to support them. For they are logically self-validating. Because it combines a naturalistic and a rationalistic conception of man to provide the basis not only for its theory of moral obligation but for its theory of the moral life in general, the view I have presented might well be called naturalistic rationalism. I would emphasize, however, that theoretically the rationalistic element is by far the more important of its two components. Besides giving the theory its distinctive character, it contributes the means by which the theory is able to solve the problem of moral knowledge.

INDEX